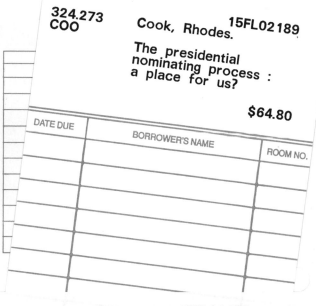

324.273
COO

Cook, Rhodes. 15FL02189

The presidential
nominating process :
a place for us?

$64.80

DATE DUE	BORROWER'S NAME	ROOM NO.

15FL02189
324.273   Cook, Rhodes.
COO
The presidential
nominating process :
a place for us?

**HAMMOND HIGH SCHOOL
HAMMOND, INDIANA**

THE PRESIDENTIAL NOMINATING PROCESS

AMERICAN POLITICAL CHALLENGES
Larry J. Sabato
Series Editor

The American political process is in trouble. Although we witnessed a movement toward specific electoral reforms in the aftermath of the 2000 election debacle, the health of our political system is still at risk. Recent events have altered the political landscape and posed new challenges, and reforms are much needed and wanted by the American public. Diligence is required, however, in examining carefully the intended and unintended consequences of reforms as we look toward the 2004 elections and beyond.

Series Editor Larry J. Sabato of the University of Virginia Center for Politics is a leading political scientist and commentator who has clear ideas about what needs to change to improve the quality of our democracy. For this series, he taps leading political authors to write cogent diagnoses and prescriptions for improving both politics and government. New and forthcoming books in the series are short, to the point, easy to understand (if difficult to implement against the political grain). They take a stand and show how to overcome obstacles to change. Authors are known for their clear writing style as well as for their political acumen.

Titles in the Series

Chesapeake Bay Blues
Science, Politics, and the Struggle to Save the Bay
   Howard R. Ernst

The Presidential Nominating Process
A Place for Us?
   Rhodes Cook

The Pursuit of Happiness in Times of War
   Carl M. Cannon

THE PRESIDENTIAL NOMINATING PROCESS

A PLACE FOR US?

RHODES COOK

ROWMAN & LITTLEFIELD PUBLISHERS, INC.
Lanham • Boulder • New York • Toronto • Oxford

ROWMAN & LITTLEFIELD PUBLISHERS, INC.

Published in the United States of America
by Rowman & Littlefield Publishers, Inc.
A wholly owned subsidiary of The Rowman & Littlefield Publishing Group, Inc.
4501 Forbes Boulevard, Suite 200, Lanham, MD 20706
www.rowmanlittlefield.com

P.O. Box 317, Oxford OX2 9RU, UK

British Library Cataloguing in Publication Information Available

Library of Congress Cataloging-in-Publication Data

Cook, Rhodes, 1948–
    The presidential nominating process : a place for us? / Rhodes Cook.
        p.   cm.— (American political challenges)
    Includes bibliographical references and index.
    ISBN 0-7425-2593-7 (cloth : alk. paper)—ISBN 0-7425-2594-5 (pbk. :
alk. paper)
    1. Presidents—United States—Nomination. I. Title. II. Series.
JK521.C625 2003
324.273′015—dc22   2003015111

Printed in the United States of America

♾ ™ The paper used in this publication meets the minimum requirements of
American National Standard for Information Sciences—Permanence of Paper for
Printed Library Materials, ANSI/NISO Z39.48–1992.

Contents

Tables and Figures

TABLES

FIGURES

Preface

Over the years, a number of books have been written about the presidential nominating process. But there is always room for one more. The process is constantly evolving from one election to another—in the number and order of the presidential primaries alone.

The goal of this book is to focus on one particular aspect—the role of voters in determining the presidential nominees—and to use that as the lens to explore other aspects of the nominating process.

In a democracy such as ours that faithfully promotes "one person, one vote," the voters should be the major players. But rarely do more than a fraction participate in the presidential primaries and caucuses, and only a small segment of those have a meaningful voice. The fortunate few are the voters in Iowa, New Hampshire, and other early-voting states that for all practical purposes decide for the rest of the nation who the nominees will be.

The thrust of this book is to discuss how we as a nation got to this point, how the nominating process currently works, and some ideas of how it might be changed in the future to give a more meaningful voice to a much larger number of voters.

Chapter 1 introduces the basic theme, "Is there a place for us?"—average voters across the country—in the important process of nominating presidential candidates.

Chapters 2 and 3 look at the history of the nominating process. Chapter 2 traces its evolution from the Founding Fathers to 1968, a span of nearly two centuries when presidential nominations went from being decided by party caucuses in Congress to national conventions, with the advent of presidential primaries early in the 20th century giving rank-and-file voters at least a bit of a say.

Chapter 3 focuses on the recent evolution of the process, from the tumultuous 1968 Democratic convention in Chicago to the present. It is a period when the number of primaries grew dramatically, and the power to nominate shifted from the conventions to the primaries—especially the early ones, where a comparatively small number of voters now ostensibly determine the nominations.

Chapter 4 explores the process in action today, from the long and increasingly important "invisible primary" season, where candidates raise money and jockey for position, to the decisive early votes in Iowa, New Hampshire, and a few other states that vote in their wake. What follows on the primary calendar is often anticlimactic, although invariably there are millions of primary ballots that remain to be cast.

Chapter 5 looks at how leading democracies in other parts of the world nominate candidates for national leadership. Six countries have been selected for study: Great Britain, France, Germany, Canada, Mexico, and Israel. In virtually every case, the nominating campaigns are shorter and less expensive than in the United States, although the nominating process in other countries usually involves an even smaller part of the electorate than here.

Chapter 6 looks to the future and the chances for reforming the nominating process in a way that would increase competition, delay the current rush to judgment, and vastly increase the number of voters with a meaningful part in selecting the presidential nominees. Although few political observers think well of the present system, change is difficult. There are a variety of power centers, competing plans, and no consensus on a course of action.

The conclusions in this book are the author's own, as are any errors in the text, for which the author takes sole responsibility. Still, this was a collaborative effort, which required the involvement of many helpful and talented people to bring it to fruition.

Larry J. Sabato planted the seed for this book and graciously included it in the series of public policy works presently being produced by the University of Virginia's Center for Politics.

Joshua J. Scott, the Center's point man on so many projects, served that role as well on this book, handling with considerable skill and alacrity preparations for production. He took on tasks that ranged from the composition of maps and graphs to the formatting of text and tables. Without his assistance, this book would probably not be done yet.

Joshua also rounded up interns at the Center to help on various aspects of research and fact-checking. My thanks to all of them, with special kudos to Catherine Giambastiani, whose extensive research on the nominating process in other countries was the basis for chapter 5. Without her dedicated work, which continued long after she graduated from the University of Virginia last year, this chapter could not have been written in anywhere near the form that it was.

Two clear-eyed readers, Prof. L. Sandy Maisel of Colby College and Rollin Radloff, a respected friend of the author, read large portions of the manuscript. Their constructive comments are deeply appreciated and hopefully are reflected accurately in this book.

At Rowman & Littlefield, executive editor Jennifer Knerr helped coax this project to conclusion with repeated words of encouragement and support that were important to hear.

And finally, my deepest thanks to my wife, Memrie McKay-Cook, who kept the home front settled as this project took on a life of its own. As she says: "You owe me!"

1

Is There a Place for Us?

Tucked away in the mountains of northern New Hampshire is the hamlet of Dixville Notch. In the dead of winter and again in the middle of the fall, its small but hearty cadre of voters assembles at midnight to cast their ballots. In wintertime, theirs are the first votes cast in the first-in-the-nation New Hampshire presidential primary. In early November, the isolated village kicks off voting in the nationwide presidential election.

Yet once the votes are tallied in Dixville Notch, the television cameras stop whirring, and the nocturnal citizenry trudges home to bed, the processes of nominating and electing the president unfold in totally different fashions.

The November balloting in Dixville Notch is followed quickly over the next 24 hours by voting across the rest of the country. And by late the following night, 100 million Americans or more have cast their ballots and the identity of the next president of the United States is usually known.

But the presidential primary schedule sprawls across the calendar from January to June, leaving uncertainty about the identities of the Democratic and Republican nominees for at least a few weeks. During the long primary season, turnout occasionally nudges 30 million, but seldom goes much higher.

There is an "Alice in Wonderland" quality to the presidential nominating process. Small states, such as New Hampshire and Iowa, enjoy an outsized influence, while large states, from New York to California, constantly struggle to find a toehold that would give them a degree of significance.

Delegates are the coin of the realm in nominating politics, and winning a majority of them brings a candidate his party's nomination. Most states these days choose their delegates through primary elections, although a few use caucuses (basically a long, multi-stage process that begins with a series of neighborhood meetings).

The rules of voter participation in these events vary from state to state. In some states, only a party's registered voters can take part. In others, independents and even voters from the other party can participate.

The American process of nominating a president is literally a world of its own, unmatched anywhere else around the globe. Compared to other countries, American nominating campaigns are costly, lengthy, and complex. And the process has proved difficult to reform. There are many players and many plans, but rarely any consensus on how to change it for the better.

Still, it is constantly evolving. The early system of congressional caucuses gave way to national conventions in the 1830s. Primaries became a part of the nominating scene in the early twentieth century, and in the 1970s primaries became so prolific in number that they have replaced the conventions as the venue where nominations are decided.

Yet whatever the era, participation in the nation's nominating process has never involved more than a comparatively small slice of the American electorate. And of late, only a small fraction of that minority has had a meaningful voice. As more and more states jockey for earlier and earlier spots on the primary calendar, nominations are being decided more quickly. And only a handful of states have much importance (see table 1.1).

Nowadays, primary voters can be divided into three groups. The most influential by far are the voters in Iowa, New Hampshire, and a few other early-voting states that shape the nominating contests and often decide them. They are the "kingmakers"—who in 2000 put Republican George W. Bush and Democrat Al Gore on the road to nomination.

Less influential are the voters in behemoths such as California, New York, and Ohio that have given the primary votefest on the first Tuesday in March the look of a "national sampler." About a dozen states voted on this day in 2000, and most of them will do so again in 2004. The last time, the voters in these states were "confirmers." They had power, because of their number, to alter the course of the nominating contests. But instead, they confirmed the advantage that the "kingmakers" had given Bush and Gore, and effectively brought down the curtain on the competitive stage of the 2000 nominating process.

With no influence at all are the voters who cast primary ballots

Table 1.1.   The Presidential Nominating Process: Few Votes Cast, Fewer Votes Matter

Barely one-half of the nation's voting-age population (18 years and older) cast ballots in the November 2000 presidential election. Less than one-third of that number participated in the presidential nominating process that produced the general election candidates.

Most of the latter (31.2 million voters) cast ballots in the Democratic and Republican presidential primaries. Several hundred thousand others participated in caucuses in the states that did not hold primaries. And roughly 2.5 million other voters cast primary ballots outside the Democratic and Republican contests.

That means the total number of participants in all aspects of the 2000 nominating process was no more than 35 million out of a nationwide voting age population of more than 200 million.

And within the pool of participants, influence varied widely. The half million or so voters who took part in the leadoff events in Iowa and New Hampshire had tremendous power in shaping the race. The millions and millions of voters who cast ballots after the nominations were decided in early March had no influence at all.

Category	Number of People
U.S. Population (2000 Census)	281,421,906
Voting Age Population (2000 Estimate)	205,814,000
Registered Voters (Nov. 2000)	159,049,775
Presidential Vote (Nov. 2000)	105,396,627
Presidential Primaries (Feb.–June 2000)	31,201,862
New Hampshire Primary (Feb. 1, 2000)	392,845
Iowa Caucuses (Jan. 24, 2000)	148,233

Source: Adapted from *America Votes 24,* 1, 42–45.

after the nominations have been decided. They are "rubber stamps," and their numbers are legion. Millions of voters in 2000 cast ballots after early March, with no opportunity at all to affect the nominating process. Their chance to participate came too late.

Altogether, barely 4 million voters who participated in the Democratic and Republican presidential primaries in 2000 were "kingmakers." Almost 14 million were "confirmers," and nearly 14 million more voters were "rubber stamps." Put another way, 12.9 percent of those who cast primary ballots in 2000 had a major role in affecting the Democratic and Republican contests; 43.6 percent had bit parts; and 43.5 percent had no part at all. They were little more than spectators.[1]

The rate of meaningful participation in the 2004 nominating process may be better. But don't bet on it. Since the last election, more states have moved their primary or caucus to February, meaning that the odds are good that both party nominations will be settled again by early March (see table 1.2 and figures 1.1, 1.2, and 1.3).

To say the current system of nominating presidential candidates is flawed is being charitable. Just as voters are becoming interested in the Democratic and Republican contests, they are abruptly over. The needed delegate majorities have been attained and the parties have quickly moved on to preparing for the fall campaigns, leaving millions of voters, almost literally, standing in line waiting to cast a primary ballot.

There are some who argue, what's wrong with that? Nominations, from president to county dogcatcher, are a party matter, they say. And it is in the parties' interest to decide their presidential nominations as quickly as possible so they can concentrate on presenting a united front for the fall election. To be sure, some of the highest turnouts for presidential primaries have come in years such as 1972 and 1984, when one of the parties was badly divided—which made for good entertainment, but bad electoral karma.

Table 1.2. Primaries and the Calendar: The Fight to Be First

Just in the last decade or two, more and more states have been holding their presidential primaries earlier and earlier in the presidential election year. The result is that a nominating process that once featured primaries sprinkled across the spring is now "front-loaded" with the bulk of the primaries held before April 1.

Following is a breakdown of the number of primaries held before and after April 1 in the first year of presidential primaries in 1912 and again since 1968, when the number of primaries began to increase dramatically. Primaries included are those in the 50 states and the District of Columbia in which at least one of the parties permitted a direct vote for presidential candidates, or there was an aggregated statewide vote for delegates.

	January–March	April–June	Total
1912	1	11	12
1968	1	14	15
1972	3	18	21
1976	6	21	27
1980	10	26	36
1984	9	21	30
1988	22	15	37
1992	17	22	39
1996	29	13	42
2000	27	16	43

Source: Adapted from *Congressional Quarterly's Guide to U.S. Elections, Volume I*, 316.

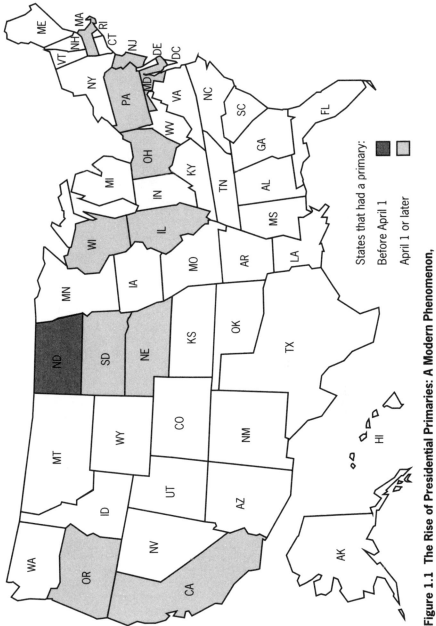

Figure 1.1 The Rise of Presidential Primaries: A Modern Phenomenon, 1912 Primaries—The Starting Point

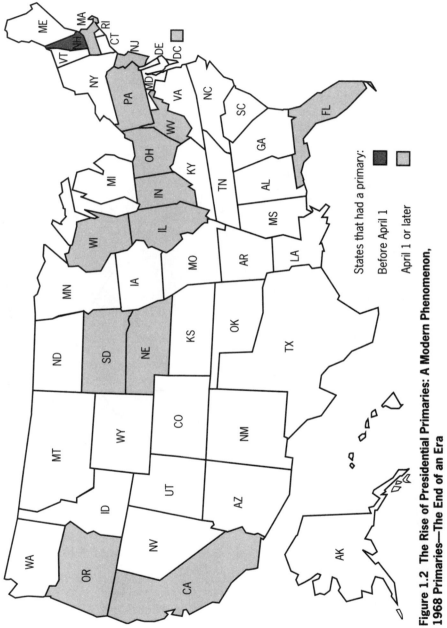

Figure 1.2 The Rise of Presidential Primaries: A Modern Phenomenon, 1968 Primaries—The End of an Era

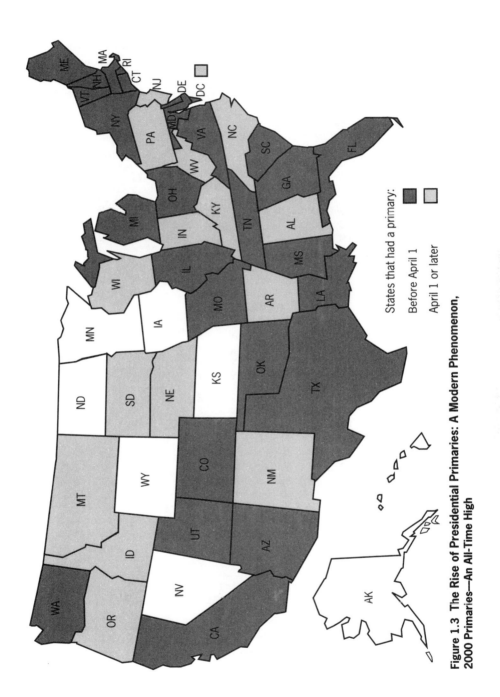

States that had a primary:

Before April 1

April 1 or later

Figure 1.3 The Rise of Presidential Primaries: A Modern Phenomenon,
2000 Primaries—An All-Time High

Table 1.3. Some Old, Some New: A Timeline of Presidential Primaries Since 1968

As recently as 1968, less than one-third of the states held presidential primaries, most of which were clustered in the Northeast and Midwest. Only two primaries that year were in the West (California and Oregon) and just one in the South (Florida). In 2000, more than 40 states held presidential primaries, including a majority in every region. In the Northeast and South, every state held a presidential primary. Recent state budget crises may force a few states to abandon their presidential primaries in

	First Primary	1968	1972	1976	1980	1984	1988	1992	1996	2000
NATIONAL		15	21	27	36	30	37	39	42	43
NORTHEAST		*6*	*8*	*9*	*11*	*11*	*11*	*10*	*13*	*13*
Connecticut	1980				X	X	X	X	X	X
Delaware	1996								X	X
District of Columbia	1952	X	X	X	X	X	X	X	X	X
Maine	1996								X	X
Maryland	1912		X	X	X	X	X	X	X	X
Massachusetts	1912	X	X	X	X	X	X	X	X	X
New Hampshire	1916	X	X	X	X	X	X	X	X	X
New Jersey	1912	X	X	X	X	X	X	X	X	X
New York	1916				X	X	X	X	X	X
Pennsylvania	1912	X	X	X	X	X	X	X	X	X
Rhode Island	1972		X	X	X	X	X	X	X	X
Vermont	1916			X	X	X	X		X	X
West Virginia	1916	X	X	X	X	X	X	X	X	X
MIDWEST		*6*	*7*	*7*	*8*	*7*	*8*	*10*	*8*	*8*
Illinois	1912	X	X	X	X	X	X	X	X	X
Indiana	1916	X	X	X	X	X	X	X	X	X
Iowa	1916									
Kansas	1980				X			X		
Michigan	1916		X	X	X			X	X	X
Minnesota	1916							X		
Missouri	1988						X			X
Nebraska	1912	X	X	X	X	X	X	X	X	X
North Dakota	1912					X	X	X	X	
Ohio	1912	X	X	X	X	X	X	X	X	X
South Dakota	1912	X	X	X	X	X	X	X	X	X
Wisconsin	1912	X	X	X	X	X	X	X	X	X

There are some who would like to see the nominating process more like the 1960s, when conventions were in their splendor and the "king-makers" were the mayors of Chicago and Pittsburgh, or the governors of New York and California. Then, results from the primaries were just one factor in the selection of a nominee as the "kingmakers" looked for a candidate who could lead the entire party ticket to victory.

2004, although at least two-thirds of the states are likely to maintain them. Primaries included below are those in the 50 states and the District of Columbia where at least one of the parties permitted a direct vote for presidential candidates, or there was an aggregated statewide vote for delegates. An asterisk (*) indicates the first year a presidential primary was held where voters in at least one party could cast a direct vote for candidates.

	First Primary	1968	1972	1976	1980	1984	1988	1992	1996	2000
SOUTH		1	3	6	11	7	13	12	12	13
Alabama	1980*				X	X	X	X	X	X
Arkansas	1976			X	X		X	X	X	X
Florida	1928	X	X	X	X	X	X	X	X	X
Georgia	1932			X	X	X	X	X	X	X
Kentucky	1976			X	X		X	X	X	X
Louisiana	1980				X	X	X	X	X	X
Mississippi	1988*				X		X	X	X	X
North Carolina	1920		X	X	X	X	X	X	X	X
Oklahoma	1988						X	X	X	X
South Carolina	1980				X		X	X	X	X
Tennessee	1972		X	X	X	X	X	X	X	X
Texas	1964				X	X	X	X	X	X
Virginia	1988						X			X
WEST		2	3	5	6	5	5	7	9	9
Alaska	—									
Arizona	1996								X	X
California	1912	X	X	X	X	X	X	X	X	X
Colorado	1992							X	X	X
Hawaii	—									
Idaho	1976			X	X	X	X	X	X	X
Montana	1916			X	X	X	X	X	X	X
Nevada	1976			X	X				X	
New Mexico	1972		X		X	X	X	X	X	X
Oregon	1912	X	X	X	X	X	X	X	X	X
Utah	2000									X
Washington	1992							X	X	X
Wyoming	—									

There are some who even look nostalgically to the days of the congressional caucus, when a party's members of Congress personally knew the strengths and weaknesses of all the candidates and selected the nominee from among them. The nominating process then placed a high value on "peer review."

Yet the clock cannot be rolled back. While arguments for past eras have merit, this is a different time—one far removed from powdered wigs and smoke-filled rooms. The political ethos of the present age exalts direct democracy and "one person, one vote." Presidential nominations made by a party elite, whether in public or behind the proverbial closed doors, would lack legitimacy in this day and age when millions and millions of voters are ready and willing to help make the choice.

There is no reason to believe that the quality of participation should decline as the quantity increases. "The more people that are involved in the nominating process, the healthier the process is," says former Republican National Committee Chairman Rich Bond.[2]

If 100 million Americans can be trusted with the task of electing the president, certainly in this day and age they should be given a meaningful voice in nominating the two candidates that realistically have the only chance of winning in November. In short, the nominating phase of the presidential election process is critical. It sets the stage for everything that follows. And there should be a place there for all of us as voters.

2

A Process in Evolution

From the Founding Fathers to 1968

Outside the animal kingdom, there may be no clearer example of Darwinism than the nation's presidential nominating system.

While the process of electing the president has remained basically the same over time—a one-day nationwide vote in early November—the practice of nominating the candidates has been constantly changing in shape and form.

The evolution has been dramatic—from congressional caucuses in the early years of the Republic to the advent of national party conventions in the early nineteenth century. In the early twentieth century, the system evolved again as a smattering of primaries began to appear, giving voters a perceptible but still advisory role. But since 1968, the primaries have grown so dramatically in number they have become the dominant feature of the nominating process and the conventions have been reduced to an afterthought.

Whether this steady progression of political Darwinism has been for the better is an open question. Even though voter input has steadily increased from one stage of the evolutionary process to another, the involvement of rank-and-file Americans in the nominating process has never been more than a fraction of those eligible to vote. And those voters with a truly meaningful voice have rarely comprised more than a small percentage of that.

Put another way, while for most of our history the process of electing a president has been democratic with a small "d," the nominating process has been mainly an insider's game. It has been controlled either by party kingmakers, or of late, by voters in a handful of states that have advantageously positioned themselves near the beginning of a bloated primary calendar.

STAGE ONE: CONGRESS NOMINATES

The Founding Fathers did not foresee the rise of political parties and there is some thought that they expected the Electoral College would be the vehicle for presidential nominations, forwarding a field of worthy candidates to the House of Representatives, which would make the final selection. Yet only the election of 1824 played out that way.[1]

Instead, the Electoral College has remained the formal method of *electing* presidents to the present day, with voter involvement steadily increasing to the point that by the late 1820s, virtually every state chose their electors by popular vote. At the same time, the nominating process quickly veered off in a different and less democratic direction.

For the first presidential election in 1789, the Electoral College in essence performed the twin roles of nominating and electing the president and vice president. There was a consensus that George Washington would be president, and he received support from all 69 electors voting. There was no consensus, though, on who should be the first vice president, and the electors widely scattered their second votes, with John Adams winning the post with 34.[2]

In the second presidential election in 1792, the semblance of a nominating process began to be seen. A small meeting of political leaders opposed to Adams met in advance of the Electoral College and selected their own candidate for vice president, Gov. George Clinton of New York. He lost, but Clinton's 'candidacy' marked the beginning of the first full-blown era in nominating politics, when national tickets would be fashioned by a small cadre of political partisans.

By the time of the third presidential election in 1796, the nominating function of the fledgling parties was assumed by its members in Congress. One of the parties, the Federalists, was to quickly decline and die in the early nineteenth century. But the other, the party of Thomas Jefferson, was to thrive and survive, and for the next quarter century its members in Congress caucused every four years to select the party's presidential candidate.

In the early years, these meetings were rather informal affairs, with the votes of the participants by secret ballot. As such, they were an appendage to the normal array of congressional activities and a pale antecedent of the modern convention, with their color and hoopla.

As Jefferson's party, often referred to (at least historically) as the Democratic-Republicans, began to dominate the national political landscape, grumbling about the congressional caucus as an appropriate nominating vehicle began to grow. To its critics, the caucus was too small in number, too elitist in character, and often too secretive in its deliberations.

And there was opposition on constitutional grounds: namely, that nominating presidential candidates was not a role for Congress, since the leader of the executive branch might ultimately feel beholden to members of the legislative branch for his position.

So evident was the grumbling that by 1808, the Democratic-Republican caucus felt compelled to defend its nominating role, approving a resolution calling the caucus "the most practicable mode of consulting and respecting the interest and wishes of all."[3]

In truth, there was a logical defense for Congress handling presidential nominations. In the nation's early years, it was the lone institution available to bring politicians together from all parts of the country. And as a practical matter, the national government at the time had fairly limited powers, so the most ambitious citizens of a political bent tended to focus their talent and energy on state and local government, where most of the action was taking place.

Even within the limited universe of Democratic-Republican members of Congress, interest in the nominating caucus was often less than intense. A corporal's guard of 43 Jeffersonian members of Congress met in Philadelphia's Marache's boardinghouse to fashion the party's national ticket in 1800. In 1804 and 1808, attendance at the Democratic-Republican nominating caucuses hovered around 100.[4]

As the young nation moved deeper into the nineteenth century, the brickbats thrown at the congressional caucus grew louder and more frequent. Pressure was building for a more active federal government. The population was increasing rapidly and the country was expanding westward. In turn, sentiment for more democratic institutions was growing. In many states, property ownership was dropped as a qualification for voting. And enough states were conducting a popular vote for presidential electors that a nationwide tally was possible by 1824.

That same year brought the coup de grace for the congressional caucus as the prime mechanism for presidential nominations, a victim of its elitist reputation and the ambitions of a variety of candidates who had little support in Congress. Barely one-quarter of the 261 Democratic-Republican members of Congress showed up for the nominating session that February and their choice, Secretary of the Treasury William Crawford, was quickly derided by his opponents as the candidate of "King Caucus."

Other major contenders were put forward by their state legislatures—John Quincy Adams by Massachusetts, Andrew Jackson by Tennessee, and Henry Clay by Kentucky. Other state legislatures made endorsements as well.[5]

Jackson finished first in the popular vote in 1824. But with no candidate winning the required majority in the Electoral College, the election was thrown into the House of Representatives where Adams emerged victorious. As for Crawford, he finished third in the electoral vote and a distant fourth in the popular vote, sounding the death knell of the congressional caucus as the nation's first presidential nominating system.

STAGE TWO: CONVENTIONS NOMINATE

The democratic impulse was increasingly evident in the popular vote for president. Nationwide, barely 365,000 ballots were cast in 1824, but the number soared past 1 million four years later, en route to the 100-million plus turnouts that have been achieved in two of the last three presidential elections (1992 and 2000) (see table 2.1).

But the nominating process moved in a more halting manner toward direct democracy. Rather than incorporate some type of national popular vote to settle presidential nominations, the parties settled on a new institution, the national convention, where delegates from each state were the coin of the realm. In most states, voters had little or no role in choosing the delegates. Primaries would not become a part of the nominating process until the early twentieth century.

The antecedents of the national convention date back to 1808, when the dying Federalist Party, bereft of enough members in Congress to hold a meaningful nominating caucus, held a secretive meeting of roughly two dozen party leaders in New York City to select their presi-

Table 2.1. Nominating the President: Never Turnouts Like the Fall

The introduction of presidential primaries in the early 20th century increased participation in the nominating process from thousands of voters to many millions. But never have the voters who turned out to nominate the parties' presidential candidates been more than a small share of those who have cast ballots in the fall presidential election.

Primary and general election turnouts are listed below for an array of key election years. Presidential primaries were initiated in a limited number of states in 1912. "N.A." indicates that precise turnouts are not available in election years before then when voter participation in the nominating process was limited to local caucuses and conventions. Never has this form of delegate selection, however, involved more than a minimal number of voters when compared to primary elections.

		Turnouts	
Election	Nominating System	Primaries	General Election
1824	Congressional Caucus, State Legislatures	N.A.	365,833
1860	Conventions	N.A.	4,685,561
1912	Conventions with Primaries	3,236,015	15,043,029
1968	Conventions with Primaries	12,008,620	73,211,875
2000	Primaries Dominant	31,201,862	105,396,627

Source: *Congressional Quarterly's Guide to U.S. Elections, Volume I,* 4, 307, 644, 653, 666.

dential candidate. In the years that followed, the convention idea gained strength at the state level, and finally burst onto the national scene in the election of 1832.[6]

Four years earlier, the candidacies of the two major contenders, Jackson and Adams, were again put forward by the legislatures of their home states. But in 1832, a new era was launched in which parties determined their presidential nominations through national conventions.

Over a span of eight months, from September 1831 to May 1832, the three parties of the day—the party soon to be known as the Democrats (headed by Jackson), the National Republicans (opposed to Jackson), and the Anti-Masons (a short-lived third party)—all held conventions in Baltimore.

The Anti-Masons went first, ensuring a place for their party in the nation's political lore. None of the initial round of conventions was contentious, since they were ratifying the selection of candidates around which a consensus had already formed. The size of the early conventions tended to reflect each state's electoral vote, with the number of delegates in the low hundreds rather than the thousands that comprise a modern convention.[7]

The Two-thirds Rule

A portentous development, though, was the Democrats' adoption of a rule requiring a two-thirds majority of delegates to win the party's presidential or vice presidential nomination. Over the next century the rule was widely regarded as a sop to the South, which was steadily losing influence as the North rapidly industrialized and gained population. Although no Southerner was picked to head the Democratic ticket from 1844 (James K. Polk of Tennessee) to 1964 (Lyndon B. Johnson of Texas), the two-thirds rule gave the region a virtual veto power over the choice of the party's nominee until the requirement was finally dropped in 1936.

The effect of the two-thirds rule was tempered a bit by the Democrats' widespread use of the unit rule (which allowed the majority within a state delegation to bind all the delegates behind their choice). Yet compared to the Republicans, which required only a simple nominating majority from their first convention in 1856 on, the Democratic gatherings were frequently long, draining and often required the selection of a compromise choice that was acceptable to most delegates but ardently supported by only a few.

More than half of the Democratic conventions held under the two-thirds rule took two or more ballots to determine a presidential nominee. Seven went more than 10 ballots, including the party's infamous 17-day marathon in 1924 that went a record 103 ballots before nominating the forgettable John W. Davis.

Meanwhile, at the same time the Democrats were laboring under the two-thirds rule, Republicans were deciding their nominees much more expeditiously. Barely one-third of the GOP conventions from 1856 through 1932 were multi-ballot affairs, and just one (in 1880) took more than 10 ballots.[8]

This proved to be the period of the Republicans' greatest ascendancy in presidential politics (see table 2.2). The Democrats won only four presidential elections from the Civil War through the 1920s, none with a majority of the popular vote. To be sure, Republicans benefited from being perceived as the "party of Lincoln" and Union in the wake of the Civil War, and the defenders of business and industry in an age of rapid economic expansion. But the Democrats' two-thirds rule was a factor as well in GOP success as it often prevented the Democrats from putting their best foot forward.

Table 2.2.   The Heyday of Conventions: Some of the Most Notable

Not since 1952 have the Democrats or Republicans taken more than one ballot to nominate their presidential candidate, but before then multi-ballot conventions were commonplace. Following is a list of the longest conventions held by the major parties as well as some other notable ones. In virtually every case, the leader on the first ballot did not ultimately win the nomination.

Most of the lengthiest conventions were held by the Democrats, who until 1936 decided their nomination on the basis of a two-thirds majority. Republicans have required only a simple majority throughout their history. Held on the eve of the Civil War, the 1860 Democratic convention in Charleston, S.C., deadlocked after 57 ballots and reconvened several weeks later in Baltimore, where Sen. Stephen Douglas of Illinois was subsequently nominated.

The Longest Conventions (10 or more ballots):

Election	Party	No. of Ballots	First Ballot Leader	Ultimate Nominee	Election Outcome
1852	Democrats	49	Lewis Cass	Franklin Pierce	Won
1852	Whigs	53	Millard Fillmore	Winfield Scott	Lost
1856	Democrats	17	James Buchanan	James Buchanan	Won
1860	Democrats	57	Stephen Douglas	(Deadlock)	Lost
1868	Democrats	22	George Pendleton	Horatio Seymour	Lost
1880	Republicans	36	Ulysses S. Grant	James Garfield	Won
1912	Democrats	46	Champ Clark	Woodrow Wilson	Won
1920	Democrats	44	William Gibbs McAdoo	James M. Cox	Lost
1920	Republicans	10	Leonard Wood	Warren Harding	Won
1924	Democrats	103	William Gibbs McAdoo	John W. Davis	Lost

Other Notable Conventions:

Election	Party	No. of Ballots	First Ballot Leader	Ultimate Nominee	Election Outcome
1860	Republicans	3	William Seward	Abraham Lincoln	Won
1896	Democrats	5	Richard Bland	William Jennings Bryan	Lost
1940	Republicans	6	Thomas Dewey	Wendell Willkie	Lost
1952	Democrats	3	Estes Kefauver	Adlai Stevenson	Lost

Source: Richard C. Bain and Judith H. Parris, *Conventions Decisions and Voting Records*, 44–292.

Democracy in Action?

The early conventions were not big affairs. No giant halls were needed. No media hordes were present. The events were small and tranquil enough to be held in small buildings, even churches or more arcane sites, such as the Egyptian Saloon on the top of Baltimore's Odd Fellows Hall (where the Democrats met in 1844).[9]

Because the means of transportation were comparatively slow throughout the nineteenth century, conventions were often held in the spring of the presidential election year in a geographically central location. Baltimore was a frequent convention host before the Civil War; Chicago emerged as a prime site in the century afterwards.

To many political observers, then and later, the convention was a logical nominating vehicle for the increasingly large and diverse republic. "The new system, the convention, gave, or so it was supposed, the mass of party members an opportunity to participate in nominations," wrote noted political scientist V. O. Key in the midst of the twentieth century. "[It was] a mechanism through which party leaders, dispersed over a nation of continental proportions, could negotiate sufficient agreement to maintain parties capable of governing through the presidential system."[10]

Conventions were much larger and more broadly based than a congressional caucus, and clearly had a wider field of vision in choosing presidential nominees. And the convention had the genius of combining several functions in one weeklong event. Not only did it nominate the party's national ticket, but adopted a party platform, settled party rules questions, and provided a place for party activists and officials from around the country to meet and discuss ways to build the party and win the upcoming election.

Yet the role of rank-and-file voters in the delegate-selection process was minimal, at best. Delegates were basically picked by two different means—state and local caucuses or conventions, or through appointment by the state party hierarchy.

At times, there could be a distinct sense of informality about delegate selection. At the Democrats' convention in Baltimore in 1835, for instance, there were 188 delegates on hand from Maryland to cast the state's 10 votes. On the other hand, a visitor from Tennessee had to be drafted to cast the Volunteer State's 15 votes.[11]

Nor were the delegates always the crème de la crème of American society. The New York delegation to the 1860 Republican convention included "a sprinkling of prize-fighters and gamblers," wrote historian George H. Mayer, a group most noteworthy for their "coarse behavior and ostentatious spending."[12]

In their heyday, conventions were hothouses of unpredictability. Without clear directives from the voters to anchor them, the proceedings were open to wheeling and dealing and quick shifts in momentum. "An institution so transient as a national convention can be unconventional in its choices," wrote Key, "a circumstance that is sometimes frightening."[13]

Not even incumbent presidents were safe in this environment. Five were denied nomination over the course of the nineteenth century—John Tyler in 1844, Millard Fillmore in 1852, Franklin Pierce in 1856, Andrew Johnson in 1868, and Chester A. Arthur in 1884. Admittedly, all but Pierce were "accidental" presidents, having assumed the presidency on the death of his predecessor. And Tyler and Johnson were not even members of the parties that nominated them for vice president.

Still, they were the only five presidents to ever be denied renomination in the nation's history. The two twentieth-century presidents who were chastened by Democratic primary voters in New Hampshire, Harry Truman (in 1952) and Lyndon Johnson (in 1968), never officially announced their candidacies before deciding that retirement was the best option.

Prior to primaries, one of the few ways voter sentiment could be heard directly was through the roar of the convention galleries. The Republican gathering in 1860 was arguably the first where the spectators had a hand in determining the outcome, although most of the people that packed the convention hall in Chicago that year were not a representative slice of "vox populi." They were there to vocally support the nomination of Illinois' own Abraham Lincoln.

Lincoln's supporters were ensured low-cost train tickets to Chicago, and many were given counterfeit tickets to get into the hall, an intimate structure 180 feet long and 100 feet wide dubbed "the Wigwam" that was specially constructed for the convention. A long-time friend of Lincoln's, Leonard Swett, wrote that when "Honest Abe's" name was placed in nomination: "Five thousand people leaped to their seats, women not wanting, and the wild yell made vesper breathings of all that preceded. A thousand steam whistles, ten acres of hotel gongs, a tribe of Comanches might have mingled in the scene unnoticed." Lincoln was nominated on the third ballot.[14]

At times, conventions were swayed by spell-binding oratory. The most famous example came during the Democratic convention of 1896, when William Jennings Bryan delivered his legendary "Cross of Gold" speech, with its peroration: "You shall not press down upon the brow of labor this crown of thorns, you shall not crucify mankind upon a cross of gold."

Wrote historian Paul Glad: "Bryan's eloquence crowded every thought out of the minds of the delegates and set reporters to groping for words. It tingled the scalp; it brought tears to the eyes; it took one's breath away."

Bryan had shown himself to be not only a great orator but also a master tactician as he scheduled himself to be the final speaker in the platform debate on the free coinage of silver, which immediately preceded the presidential balloting. In one speech, the 36-year-old "boy orator of the Platte" was able to elevate himself from the ranks of the long shots into the top tier of contenders for the Democratic presidential nomination. Bryan was subsequently nominated on the fifth ballot, the first of three nominations he would receive from the Democratic Party.[15]

A number of conventions during the nineteenth and early twentieth centuries, though, were decided by the mundane matter of who controlled the chair, with the right to interpret convention rules and recognize (or not recognize) motions from the floor. The course of more than one convention was determined at its outset on the vote for temporary chairman. And candidates often augmented the surface competition with horse-trading, gamesmanship, and out and out shenanigans.

Typical of the latter was a suspicious episode at the 1876 Republican convention. Shortly after former House Speaker James G. Blaine was nominated in an eloquent speech that hailed him as the "plumed knight," the gas lights in the hall suddenly failed. No one knows for certain whether it was coincidence or the work of a rival candidate. But rather than begin the balloting for president, the convention was forced to adjourn until the next day and Blaine's momentum ebbed. He was not to win the Republican nomination until eight years later.[16]

With a few notable exceptions, conventions throughout the nineteenth century were not so divisive that they prevented the Democrats or Republicans from putting up a united front for the fall election.

But as the century wound down, there was a growing perception that the proceedings were controlled by party bosses and their special interest allies. Wrote the *Emporia* (Kans.) *Gazette*'s legendary publisher William Allen White of the 1896 Republican convention: "The applause is hollow; the enthusiasm dreary and the delegates sit like hogs in a car and know nothing about anything."[17]

White reflected a viewpoint that was gaining currency. The time was ripe for a new mechanism that would provide broader and more direct voter participation in the presidential nominating process.

STAGE THREE: THE RISE OF PRIMARIES

Ironically, the concept of presidential primaries dates back before the Civil War to John C. Calhoun of South Carolina. While he has lived in history as one of the most visceral opponents of the era's premier grassroots "democrat," Andrew Jackson, Calhoun was also an early champion of primaries for delegate selection.

At one point, he suggested that voters directly elect delegates by congressional district, rather than have the choice controlled by state party leaders or the small universe of party activists that they influenced. Calhoun's concept of presidential primaries reflected his belief in protecting individual and minority rights, although it was also designed to promote his uphill presidential ambitions, which were never realized.[18]

When the thought of presidential primaries emerged again in the early twentieth century, it was as part of a full-blown package of electoral reforms that included calls for the secret ballot, the initiative and referendum, and the direct election of senators (which were chosen by state legislatures until 1913). All of these measures were at the heart of the Progressive movement, and were designed to cleanse what was widely viewed as a corrupt electoral process by dramatically increasing the role of rank-and-file voters.

Presidential primaries appeared gradually on the political radar screen in the first decade of the twentieth century, with each region of the country playing a role in their initial development.

Florida is given credit for starting the ball rolling, enacting legislation in 1901 that gave officials in the state's dominant Democratic Party the right to hold a primary to elect national convention delegates.

Four years later, Wisconsin went a step further, calling for the election of Democratic and Republican delegates in primary elections.

Pennsylvania advanced the primary still further, passing legislation in 1906 allowing candidates for delegate to place the name of their presidential preference on a primary ballot.

And in 1910, Oregon voters approved a ballot measure establishing a primary with both a preference vote for presidential candidates and the election of delegates pledged to support the winning candidate.

1912: A "Titanic" Start for the Primaries

By early 1912, seven states had enacted legislation establishing presidential primaries with either a preference vote, the direct election of delegates, or a combination of the two. Five other states added primaries in short order, spurred by the heated contest between President William Howard Taft and former President Theodore Roosevelt for the Republican nomination.[19]

It was a passionate struggle writ large between two old friends whose political ambitions and differing beliefs on the role of government led to a legendary estrangement. Declaring late that February that "my hat is in the ring," Roosevelt launched his bid to unseat his hand-picked successor.

Even though the national convention was four months off, the GOP delegate selection process was already well under way. Taft's strength in the South, where Republican state parties were heavily dependent on federal patronage, as well as the non-primary states that had begun the process of selecting delegates before Roosevelt's campaign had geared up, put the former president at an immediate disadvantage.

Roosevelt quickly saw that his only hope was to beat Taft in as many primaries as possible, in an effort to demonstrate his broader popularity among Republican voters and his greater electability in the fall.

In early March, the Roosevelt campaign challenged Taft to compete in a nationwide primary vote. Already well ahead in the delegate count and dubious about their candidate's chances in a popularity contest with the ebullient Teddy, the Taft forces declined. Meanwhile, in league with progressive Republican elements across the Frost Belt, the Roosevelt team did what they could to quickly create primaries in as many states as they could.[20]

In some states, presidential primaries were literally created on the fly. In Illinois, the law creating it was enacted just five days before the event itself was to be held. The flurry of activity required to birth the event was vividly described in the April 5 edition of the *Illinois State Register*: "Having been previously adopted by the Illinois senate, the legislation was 'passed by the house; signed by Speaker Adkins at 11:15; signed by President Oglesby of the senate at 11:30; rushed to the attorney general's office for his inspection; conveyed to Governor Deneen who was ill at mansion and there signed by him at 3:25 p.m.'" Barely an hour later, the Taft campaign filed nominating petitions to get on the Illinois primary ballot.[21]

The initial set of primaries spanned the country's northern tier from Massachusetts to California. Six were in the Midwest (Illinois, Ohio and Wisconsin, and the Plains states of Nebraska, North Dakota and South Dakota). Four were in the Northeast (Maryland, Massachusetts, New Jersey and Pennsylvania). Two were on the Pacific Coast (California and Oregon).

Altogether, there were presidential primaries in 12 states, with Republicans also holding a delegate-selection primary in parts of New York that did not produce a statewide tally. None of the initial primaries, though, was in the South and only Maryland's was located below the Mason-Dixon line. As for Iowa and New Hampshire, the gatekeepers of the modern nominating process, they held their first presidential primaries in 1916.

The initial round of primaries in 1912 (see table 2.3 and figure 2.1) was scattered across the calendar from mid-March to early June. North Dakota launched the year's primary action on March 19; South Dakota concluded it on June 4, with six primary contests in April and four in May sandwiched in between.

For both candidates and reporters, it was quickly evident that the presidential nominating process was vastly different than it had been just four years earlier. "All the old political traditions have been broken wide open this year," wrote a *New York Times* reporter in early April.[22]

No one quite knew what to make of it. In typical fashion, Roosevelt threw himself into an energetic blur of cross-country campaigning. It was not unusual for him to make 10 or 15 speeches a day, many from his railroad train as it passed through hamlets and small towns.

Meanwhile, at least at the start, Taft tended to follow the "above the fray" manner of an earlier era. Like Republican nominee William McKinley in 1896, who made only one speech all year outside his hometown of Canton, Ohio, Taft tended to stay close to the White House in an early version of the "Rose Garden" strategy.[23]

So laid back was Taft in the early going that about all the White House could report one mild April day was that the president had taken the afternoon off to play golf. But the peripatetic Teddy was soon to change Taft's mood of complacency with a landslide victory in the Illinois primary April 9. The result immediately changed the perception of the race from a Taft cakewalk to a nip and tuck competition that forced the rotund president onto the stump.

Although Taft and Roosevelt had been close friends when the former served in TR's Cabinet as secretary of war, it was not long before each became quite tart-tongued in criticizing the other. To Roosevelt, Taft was "a fathead" and a "puzzle-wit" who had "brains less than those of a guinea-pig." For his part, Taft labeled his former boss as "a

Table 2.3.   There at the Start: The Primaries of 1912

When presidential primaries were initiated on a nationwide scale in 1912, there were only 12 of them. But the initial group included many of the larger states—Massachusetts, New Jersey, and Pennsylvania in the Northeast; Illinois, Ohio, and Wisconsin in the Midwest; and California in the West. New York Republicans held a primary for the election of some congressional district delegates but there was no statewide tally.

More than 3 million voters participated in the primaries of 1912, most on the Republican side where President William Howard Taft was challenged by former President Theodore Roosevelt. TR dominated the primaries but lost the nomination to Taft, who controlled the party machinery and most of the GOP delegates from non-primary states.

Still, the primaries were a hit at the ballot box. Voter turnout in the dozen states that held primaries was 52 percent of the fall general election turnout, reaching 80 percent in the year's leadoff primary in North Dakota. By comparison, turnout for the first-in-the-nation New Hampshire primary in 2000 was 69 percent of the votes cast that November.

The electorate in 1912 was limited to men, mainly white men. Women were not given the right to vote until 1920. An asterisk (*) indicates that the Pennsylvania primary vote in 1912 was based on unofficial returns.

State	Primary Date	Primaries	General	Primary Turnout as % of General Election Turnout
North Dakota	March 19	69,025	86,474	80%
Wisconsin	April 2	264,696	399,975	66%
Illinois	April 9	731,100	1,146,173	64%
Pennsylvania	April 13	572,032*	1,217,736	47%
Nebraska	April 19	129,226	249,483	52%
Oregon	April 19	90,027	137,040	66%
Massachusetts	April 30	222,182	488,056	46%
Maryland	May 6	117,700	231,981	51%
California	May 14	314,161	677,877	46%
Ohio	May 21	485,857	1,037,114	47%
New Jersey	May 28	157,653	433,663	36%
South Dakota	June 4	82,356	116,327	71%

Source: *Congressional Quarterly's Guide to U.S. Elections, Volume I,* 320–21, 666; James W. Davis, *Springboard to the White House,* 278–79.

dangerous egotist," a "demagogue," and a politician who "could not tell the truth." As for his own newfound pugnacity, Taft noted none too elegantly that "even a rat in a corner will fight."[24]

The sinking of the "unsinkable" *Titanic* in the darkness of the icy North Atlantic April 15 caused a sensation that gripped the country for weeks. But the Taft-Roosevelt battle had a sensational quality of its own, and it was hard to keep it off the front pages of the nation's newspapers for long.

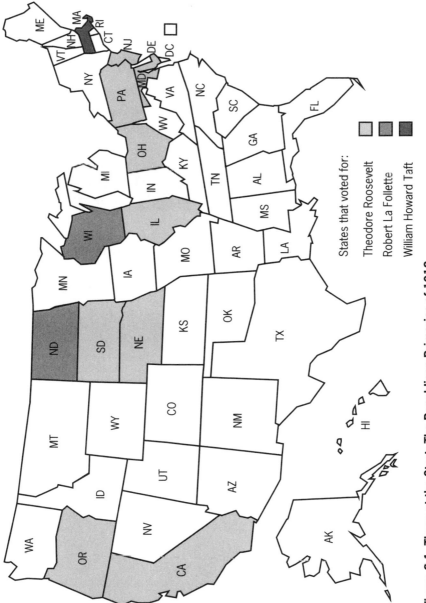

States that voted for:

Theodore Roosevelt
Robert La Follette
William Howard Taft

Figure 2.1 There at the Start: The Republican Primaries of 1912

In its nastiness, the Taft-Roosevelt battle was a precursor of the sharp-elbowed nominating campaigns of modern times. Yet both candidates also defined in detail their philosophical differences, with Roosevelt championing a proactive brand of progressivism that he called "the new nationalism," while Taft favored consolidation of legislative gains that had already been made.

The appearance of a clear choice, coupled with the lively action, captivated and engaged the populace. Crowds were large for their speeches and so were the primary turnouts. Yet the result in virtually state after state was the same, a clear-cut Roosevelt victory.

He crushed Taft by a margin in the vicinity of 30 percentage points in Illinois and California, by 20 points in Pennsylvania, and by 15 points in New Jersey and Taft's home state of Ohio. Altogether, Roosevelt defeated Taft in nine of the 10 primaries where the two went head to head, with the incumbent's lone victory in Massachusetts by the narrow margin of 2 percentage points.

Of the two and one-quarter million votes cast in the 12 Republican primaries, Roosevelt won 400,000 votes more than Taft, taking 52 percent of the GOP primary ballots to the president's 34 percent. Most of the remaining votes went to Sen. Robert La Follette, who won the year's other two primaries in North Dakota and his home state of Wisconsin.[25]

Yet though he was trounced in the primaries, Taft had several aces up his sleeve that trumped Roosevelt's ballot box appeal. Since there were comparatively few primaries, Taft's strength among party loyalists in non-primary states gave him a tenuous edge in the nationwide delegate count. And Taft forces controlled the Republican National Committee, which organized the convention in Chicago and made initial determinations on the myriad credentials challenges brought against Taft delegates by the Roosevelt forces. The committee's decisions were almost unanimous in favor of Taft and set the tone for the convention that followed.

The convention hall itself was readied quite literally for pitched combat. Barbed wire was concealed in the patriotic bunting around the podium and extra police were detailed to the hall. But the Taft forces gained firm control of the proceedings by narrowly winning the contest for temporary chairman and the series of credentials challenges that followed. In response, the Roosevelt delegates elected to make their protest a largely silent one.[26]

There were occasional shouts of "liar, liar" and "pack of thieves," as well as noise from Roosevelt supporters in the galleries rubbing sandpaper and tooting horns to emulate the sound of a steamroller. But on the floor, realizing their cause was lost, Roosevelt delegates simply abstained from voting, until they finally left the hall to join their candidate in a mass meeting that lay the groundwork for the new Progressive Party.[27]

Setting a Tone

The nation's first go-round with presidential primaries received mixed reviews. On the down side, the bitter nature of the highly visible Republican primary contest helped produce the first significant election-year division within a major party since the Democrats split asunder in 1860 on the eve of the Civil War.

Primaries also forced the nominees of each party to run two full-blown campaigns—one for the nomination and one for the general election, with the result not only increased intraparty friction but a significant increase in the price of running for president. Taft and Roosevelt together spent more than $1 million in pursuit of the Republican nomination, a considerable sum by 1912 standards.[28]

And to the chagrin of both parties, the primaries removed a portion of their control over the nominating process. The power of candidates to fashion their own destiny was enhanced, as was the role of the communications industry—first, newspapers and magazines; in later years, radio and television.

Yet there was no denying that with primaries, a nominating process that had previously involved thousands of voters, now engaged millions. As well as the two and a quarter million votes counted in the Republican primaries, nearly a million more voters participated in the Democratic contests, dividing their ballots mainly between New Jersey Gov. Woodrow Wilson and House Speaker Champ Clark of Missouri.

The combined turnout for the dozen Democratic and Republican primaries in 1912 comprised more than half the number that cast ballots in those same states in the fall presidential election—a much higher rate of participation than nowadays, when only a handful of presidential primaries are truly meaningful.[29]

In several important ways, the 1912 Taft-Roosevelt fight set the tone for presidential nominating contests to follow.

First, it showed that people would vote in goodly numbers when they felt they had something meaningful to vote for and were given the chance to do so.

Second, it vividly demonstrated that the candidate that controlled the party machinery had a strong advantage, regardless of the primary vote. It would not be until the 1970s that enough delegates were elected in primaries to enable a candidate to successfully circumvent the party hierarchy.

And third, the GOP nominating contest of 1912 showed that a poor showing by a nominee in his party's primaries is almost always a harbinger of problems in the fall. For Taft, they turned out to be huge problems, as he ran a distant third behind both Wilson and Roosevelt in both the popular and electoral vote.

Not surprisingly, Roosevelt's Progressive Party included a platform plank calling for the adoption of nationwide primaries. So too did the platform of the Democratic Party, which nominated Wilson on the 46th ballot.[30]

With the Republicans badly divided, Wilson was elected that fall. And in his first annual message to Congress in 1913, he advocated that presidential primaries replace conventions as the parties' prime nominating mechanism. "I feel confident," said Wilson, "that I do not misinterpret the wishes or the expectations of the country when I urge the prompt enactment of legislation which will provide for primary elections throughout the country at which voters of several parties may choose their nominees for the presidency without the intervention of nominating conventions." In Wilson's view, conventions of the future could focus on drawing up the party platform.[31]

But the moment for bold change passed quickly. The idea of broadly democratizing the presidential nominating process dropped off the radar screen as the Progressive movement ebbed and the nation's involvement in World War I drew closer.

Back to Normalcy

Nine more states added presidential primaries between 1912 and 1916, bringing the total to 20. But that proved to be the high-water mark of this first attempt to dramatically open the presidential nominating process to grass-roots participation. Without either reform sentiment or highly competitive races to sustain them, the number of primaries began to ebb, as many states put their contests into mothballs.[32]

Over the next quarter century, some presidential candidates continued to use the primaries that remained to demonstrate their personal popularity, although head-to-head contests between major contenders were rare and personal campaigning by front-tier candidates in the primaries was virtually nil. Warren Harding's observation during the 1920 campaign that it was time for "a return to normalcy" applied to the presidential nominating process as well, with the national conventions at center stage, party leaders directing the action, and the primaries no more than bit players in the whole production.

This period was to last until World War II. Party leaders were quite happy to see the primaries go into eclipse. Many states were eager to save the money that a presidential primary cost to conduct, particularly when held independently of their state primaries. And candidates felt free to either avoid the primaries altogether or to pick and choose the contests they wished to enter.

New York Gov. Franklin D. Roosevelt, for instance, skillfully used the primaries in 1932 to circumvent opposition from a number of Democratic leaders in the Northeast still loyal to the party's 1928 nominee, Al Smith. FDR put his name on the ballot in primaries across the country, scoring early victories in North Dakota and Georgia (where he had already introduced himself to voters through his convalescent visits to Warm Springs to seek therapy for polio). His victories at the ballot box set the tone for a successful drive that led to his fourth-ballot nomination. Yet FDR did not personally campaign in any of the primary states and often did not face more than token opposition.[33]

Meanwhile, Supreme Court Justice Charles Evans Hughes captured the Republican nomination in 1916 without campaigning for the nomination at all. Warren Harding was nominated four years later after entering the GOP convention as little more than a "favorite son" candidate. Harding had entered only two primaries that spring, narrowly winning in his home state of Ohio, while finishing fourth out of a field of four in neighboring Indiana. Wendell Willkie won the Republican nomination in 1940 without entering a single primary.

Some individual primary contests during this period were fascinating in their own way. When pursuing the Democratic nomination in 1928, Smith (a Catholic from New York City) ran against Sen. James Reed (a Protestant from Missouri) in the West Virginia primary. It turned out to be a low-budget precursor of the epic contest between Sens. John Kennedy and Hubert Humphrey in the Mountaineer State 32 years later. Smith reported spending $4,265 to narrowly win the West Virginia primary; Reed put his primary expenditures at $41.[34]

Millions of voters still cast primary ballots during this period between the wars, but their votes tended to be much less meaningful than in the initial round of primaries in 1912. From the eve of World War I to the brink of World War II, the primaries had whatever value the party leaders gave them, which usually was not much. Not surprisingly, the proportion of voters involved in the nominating process fell after 1912. Between 1912 and 1952, the number of votes cast in the limited number of primary states never exceeded 20 percent of the nationwide vote cast for president in the fall.

Conventions were still in their heyday then, but clearly they were not always models of efficiency or democracy. Three out of the four Democratic gatherings between 1912 and 1924 took more than 40 ballots to choose a nominee. The Republican convention in 1920 ran 10 ballots, capped by a late-night meeting in a "smoke-filled room," when, legend has it, a cabal of Senate leaders tipped the nomination to Harding, their Senate colleague.

Yet the era in which surface chaos and backroom deal making could thrive in a convention environment was gradually coming to an end. The advent of radio in the early 1920s allowed voters to hear for the first time the excitement and drama of the conventions, as well as the voices of dissent and the puerile shenanigans. It did not always make for good listening.

Unfortunately for the Democrats, the first convention covered by radio on a gavel-to-gavel basis was their epic gathering in New York's old Madison Square Garden in 1924. The convention got under way with a tense platform fight over condemnation of the Ku Klux Klan, which was rejected by a margin of less than one vote, and concluded with 103 mind-numbing ballots for president.[35]

As is so often the case after unruly conventions, the Democrats' marathon 1924 gathering left many voters doubting whether a party that had so much trouble governing itself could govern the country. In the three-way presidential election that fall, the Democrats' compromise candidate, John W. Davis, took just 29 percent of the popular vote, the party's lowest share of the presidential vote ever.

The longest convention since then went six ballots, the 1940 Republican gathering that nominated Willkie. One of history's most famous dark-horse candidates, Willkie went from being a blip on the political radar screen to the GOP presidential nomination in a matter of weeks. A wealthy utilities lawyer with an international outlook on foreign affairs, Willkie was aided by a friendly, "aw, shucks" manner, an astute management team with ties to the national media, and convention galleries packed with supporters that incessantly chanted, "We want Willkie!"

Entering the contest too late to participate in the primaries, Willkie relied instead on a newfangled measurement of voter opinion, the public opinion poll, to give his candidacy needed credibility. The scientific polling, as practiced by George Gallup and his colleagues, had gained immediate acceptance in 1936, when it successfully predicted the reelection of Franklin D. Roosevelt. In the weeks leading up to the 1940 Republican convention, the Gallup Poll tracked Willkie's rise from a virtual unknown to the top tier of candidates favored by Republican voters.[36]

THE PRIMARIES: ON THE MAP FOR GOOD

But Willkie, a one-time Democrat, was never a favorite of GOP leaders. After running a respectable but losing race against FDR in 1940, Willkie gauged that his only hope of winning the Republican nomination again was through the primaries.

From the start of his 1944 campaign, Willkie campaigned as a consummate "outsider." He attacked the anti-New Deal core of the Republican Party, called for an election-year tax increase, and chose Wisconsin—one of the most isolationist states in the country—to mount the ultimate test of his candidacy. The odds were long, but Willkie campaigned with gusto. "Never before had a national political figure of his stature invested so much energy and time in a single primary," wrote political writer Steve Neal in a biography of Willkie.[37]

Willkie spent nearly two weeks barnstorming across Wisconsin, usually in a caravan of 1942 Dodges, but once in a horse-drawn sleigh when weather conditions deteriorated. By the time of the state's April primary, Willkie had made scores of speeches to what the candidate estimated to be more than 70,000 Wisconsin voters.[38]

As the only major candidate to campaign in the state, Willkie hoped to make a virtue of his presence. But it was cancelled out by a feeling among many rank-and-file Republicans that Willkie was a "Carbon Copy Roosevelt." The Wisconsin primary results proved a disaster for his comeback bid, as he failed to win a single delegate and drew less than 5 percent of the separate preference vote. The next day he quit the race.[39]

But Willkie had nudged the presidential nominating process in a new direction. His campaign in Wisconsin launched an era where candidates would personally campaign for support in the primaries, giving voters in at least a few states a direct voice in selecting party nominees. At first, it was political outsiders who took the "primary route" as a way to impress party leaders with their vote-getting appeal. But gradually over the next quarter century, it became mandatory for all presidential aspirants to contest at least some of the primaries.

New York Gov. Thomas Dewey had beaten Willkie in Wisconsin, and gone on to win the Republican nomination in 1944 the "old fashioned way," by remaining detached from the grass-roots action while leaving the work of his campaign to party professionals and political allies. But four years later, Dewey found himself in a position similar to Willkie's in 1944—a defeated nominee forced to use the primaries as the route to a second chance at the White House.

Dewey was better positioned than Willkie to make a successful run. He had a better organization, was better networked with Republican leaders, and had a strong base in what was then the nation's most populous state.

Still, Dewey needed a high-profile primary victory to demonstrate his continued popularity among Republican voters, and was forced into a high-stakes contest with former Minnesota Gov. Harold Stassen in Oregon.

Their primary battle proved a prototype of the type of campaigning that is accorded only a few primary states each election cycle. Both candidates stumped the state for days. Expenses, jacked up by radio advertising, were heavy for the time—reportedly in the vicinity of $100,000 for each candidate. And for the first time in a presidential primary, a face-to-face debate between the leading candidates was held, and proved a major factor in the outcome.

The debate, carried nationwide by radio, focused on the issue of whether the Communist Party should be outlawed in the United States. Stassen argued yes; Dewey argued no, claiming that it would be easier to track Communists if the party was legal. Most observers believed that Dewey won the debate.

But equally important in the primary outcome was Dewey's effort to soften his public image. Long regarded as stiff as a plastic man on top of a wedding cake, Dewey exuded a rarely seen folksiness. Wrote a correspondent for *Time*: "He peered at cows in Corvallis, at logging operations along the Umpqua River. He accepted a salmon at Oregon City, signed his name in blood for a local booster club at Coos Bay, paraded with an organization called the "Cavemen" at Grants Pass and, at their bidding, munched on a large bone." Added *Newsweek*: "No trick was too corny for the new Dewey."[40]

The "new Dewey" won the Oregon primary by less than 10,000 votes out of more than 225,000 cast. But it was enough to propel him toward the Republican nomination in 1948.

Another success story was the primary itself, as it was clear that the lively, grass-roots campaigning had engaged Oregon voters. Turnout was far larger than any previous presidential primary in the state, Republican or Democratic. And the combined number of votes cast in Oregon in both parties' presidential primaries in 1948 was almost two-thirds the number that cast ballots in the presidential election that fall, an unusually high percentage.

Taft vs. Eisenhower: Hints of 1912

The Republican nominating campaign of 1952 was similar in many respects to that 40 years earlier, with Sen. Robert Taft of Ohio reprising the part of his father, William Howard Taft, and Dwight D. Eisenhower the role of Teddy Roosevelt. To be sure, neither had served as president like the two principals in 1912. But as the GOP leader in the Senate and a long-time foe of accommodation with the Democrats, Taft was widely known as "Mr. Republican" and was a favorite of much of the conservative party establishment that had backed his father a generation earlier.

In terms of his resume, Eisenhower was the antithesis of Taft. He had never before run for office and did not even allow he was a Republican until January 1952. Yet as leader of the Allied forces in Europe during World War II, Ike was one of the most respected and popular figures in the country. And he counted on a strong showing in the primaries to give his campaign credibility.

He got off to a strong start, beating Taft by more than 10 percentage points in the lead-off contest in New Hampshire and following it with a hastily organized 100,000-vote write-in showing in the Gopher

State that the media dubbed the "Miracle of Minnesota." Ike's vote-getting ability was considered even more spectacular since he was an absentee candidate, based in Paris through the spring as the Supreme Commander of the North Atlantic Treaty Organization (NATO).[41]

Yet for all his appeal, Eisenhower did not dominate the Republican primaries in 1952 as completely as Roosevelt had in 1912. In only a few primary contests were Taft and Eisenhower actually listed on the ballot together. And Taft swept virtually all the primaries in his native Midwest, including South Dakota, where he edged Ike in the party's final primary of the year.

But Eisenhower had three big assets that TR did not have 40 years earlier. First, public opinion polls showed him a surer bet to win in November than Taft, with coattails that could boost the entire GOP ticket. Second, Republican governors were almost unanimously on Ike's side, offering him potent organizational support that offset Taft's base among fellow members of Congress and the party hierarchy. And third, as opposed to the frequently dour-looking Taft, the affable, smiling former military leader was a natural match for the nation's rapidly growing new medium of choice, television.[42]

Taft entered the Republican convention in 1952 in a similar position to his father in 1912—with a tenuous lead in the delegate count and control of the party machinery. But under the glare of the TV lights, Taft's advantage quickly melted away. All of the major decisions that had gone his father's way went against the son.

Buoyed by support from uncommitted delegates, the Eisenhower forces pushed through a "fair play amendment" that prevented delegates whose credentials were challenged from voting on any credentials contest, then won a series of challenges that favorably positioned Eisenhower to capture the nomination.[43]

As in 1912, turnout for the primaries in 1952 had been strong in the states that held them. The number of votes cast in the Republican primaries approached 8 million, nearly double the previous high. On the Democratic side turnout approached 5 million, the party's second-highest total up to that time. But as before, the level of voter participation was limited by the small number of primaries—just 16 for the Democrats and 13 for the Republicans. The nearly 13 million primary voters represented barely 20 percent of the number that participated in the presidential election that fall.

Yet the Republican contest did show the increasing influence of primaries. For the first time, a candidate that depended heavily on a strong primary showing won a hard fought battle for his party's nomination. But the Democratic contest in 1952 showed that unless a candidate enjoyed the unique stature of an Eisenhower, he still needed to combine strength in the primaries with considerable support from party leaders.

Sen. Estes Kefauver of Tennessee was more dominant in the Democratic primaries of 1952 than Eisenhower in the Republican contests. He upset President Truman in the New Hampshire primary, then went on to win virtually every primary that followed. Yet Kefauver's win in the Granite State, as eye-catching as it was, proved to be a Pyrrhic victory. Although Truman's name was on the ballot, he did not campaign in New Hampshire and had not even declared his candidacy. In winning there, Kefauver drew the president's ire while leaving the senator with no giant to slay in the remaining primaries.

Kefauver's problem was evident immediately after his big New Hampshire win. "All delegates elected or instructed by primary ballot are no more than a splash in the bucket," wrote *Newsweek*. "The consensus among Democrats was that Mr. Truman, low as his political fortunes had fallen, could have the nomination if he wanted it and could prevent the nomination of anyone he didn't want, including Kefauver."[44]

That, in truth, came to pass. Although Kefauver garnered nearly two-thirds of the Democratic primary ballots in 1952, he had less than one-third of the delegates at the party's national convention. Illinois Gov. Adlai Stevenson, who had skipped the primaries, was nominated on the third ballot—with Truman's blessing.

Truman had dismissed the primaries as "eyewash" and Stevenson was not a big fan of them either. But losing to Ike in 1952 and wanting a rematch, Stevenson believed that he had to enter at least a few of the primaries in 1956 to show that he was still the choice of his party's voters. He adopted a "Four Corners'" strategy of sorts, focusing on a single primary in each region of the country.[45]

Stevenson's execution was not flawless. He lost to Kefauver in Minnesota and was essentially unopposed in Pennsylvania. But he finished strong, defeating Kefauver narrowly in Florida and by a wide margin in California. Stevenson went on to win the Democratic nomination on the first ballot.

The 1952 Democratic convention was the last of either major party to take more than one ballot to nominate a candidate for president. The

Democratic convention four years later was the last to take more than a single ballot to nominate a candidate for vice president.

Rather than naming his own running mate, Stevenson in 1956 left the choice to the convention. His decision created confusion and drama within the convention hall that would be witnessed live by millions of Americans on their relatively new black-and-white TV sets.

Kefauver took the lead on the first ballot, followed by John F. Kennedy (JFK) and Tennessee's other senator, Al Gore (the father of the Democrats' 2000 presidential candidate). On the second ballot, the race narrowed to Kennedy and Kefauver, with the latter winning the vice presidential nomination after a late flurry of vote changes at the end of the roll call.

The dramatic ending gave the young senator from Massachusetts the opportunity to mount the podium and graciously concede the number two spot on the ticket to Kefauver, as well as to unofficially launch his own bid for the Democratic presidential nomination in 1960.

The Romanticizing of the Primaries

As it turned out, the Kennedy campaign was one of the most memorable in American history. It began with an intriguing candidate. JFK was a war hero, an Ivy League graduate, the scion of a wealthy Irish-American family, a Pulitzer Prize-winning author and U.S. senator.

But he was also a Roman Catholic in a nation that had never before elected a Catholic president. Kennedy needed to prove in the primaries to the Democratic bosses, many of them Catholic themselves, that his religion was not a disqualifying factor. The fact that he felt he needed to win every primary that he entered gave a high-stakes quality to his campaign.

With its cool efficiency and aura of glamour, the Kennedy campaign made stars of many of the political journalists that covered it—none more so than Theodore H. White. After the election, White wrote a Pulitzer Prize-winning book of his own, *The Making of the President 1960*. Combining a flair for detail and analysis with a storyteller's grace, White painted the campaign in lyrical terms, devoting a chapter to Kennedy's primary victories in Wisconsin and West Virginia.

Kennedy won in Wisconsin over his most prominent primary rival, Minnesota's Hubert Humphrey, but not by an overwhelming margin. Kennedy rolled up a big lead in the Catholic areas of the state while losing the Protestant areas.[46]

That raised the stakes for Kennedy in heavily Protestant West Virginia, where he decided to meet the religious issue head on. "I refuse to believe that I was denied the right to be president on the day I was baptized," he said. And with a campaign rich in manpower and financial resources, Kennedy had the underfunded Humphrey outmatched.[47]

In retrospect, Kennedy's victory in West Virginia by the decisive margin of 3-to-2 was a logical outcome. But as primary day in the Mountaineer State approached that early May in 1960, the result was considered too close to call. That it turned out to be a Kennedy landslide was vividly described by White in his "you are there" description of the election night tally: "By ten o'clock the (Kennedy) sweep was no longer spotty but statewide. . . . Hill pocket, hill slope, industrial town, Charleston, Parkersburg, Wheeling, suburb, white, Negro—the Kennedy tide was moving, powerfully, irresistibly, all across the Protestant state, writing its message for every politician in the nation to see. There remained then only the ceremonies of burial for the Humphrey candidacy and of triumph for Kennedy."[48]

In actual numbers, there were no more presidential primaries in 1960 than usual—a total of just 16 on the Democratic side. But with White's help, these scattered tappings of the national electorate were to take on a romantic aura, which was to characterize coverage of the primaries throughout the 1960s.

Primary campaigning proved to be a perfect match for the visual medium of television. And by 1964, the major networks were devoting blocks of time on primary election nights to discuss and analyze the results. Meanwhile, candidates that skipped the action were increasingly in danger of having their manhood challenged.

Adding to the growing interest in the primaries was the turbulent backdrop of the decade—from the assassination of President Kennedy in November 1963, through the turmoil over civil rights at mid-decade, to the Vietnam War, which dominated political discourse in the late 1960s. The primaries proved a colorful venue for the issues to be engaged.

And just as events were writ large, so were the presidential nominating contests. In 1964, Sen. Barry Goldwater of Arizona led a conservative takeover of the Republican Party that has held to this day. Ironically, though, Goldwater was never very popular among Republican voters during that critical nominating season. The Gallup Poll showed him to be the favorite of only 20 percent of the GOP rank and file at the beginning of the 1964 primary season, and of just 22 percent five months later on the eve of his nomination.[49]

But Goldwater possessed a cadre of zealous supporters that were able to dominate delegate-selection contests in the myriad low-turnout caucus states that provided him with a solid core of delegates. And a critical win in California at the end of the primary season put Goldwater in favorable position to win the nomination.

His California victory was not a landslide by any means. It was his strong showing in the burgeoning suburbs of Southern California that pushed him past New York Gov. Nelson Rockefeller by less than 70,000 votes out of nearly 2.2 million cast. But it was a winner-take-all primary, giving Goldwater the delegates that he needed to nail down the nomination.

"Goldwater had won only one contested primary," wrote White, "and that by a scanty margin in a state unique in feel and longings. It was power, though." And with it, Goldwater and his supporters were able to impose a new Sun Belt conservatism on the Republican Party.[50]

In 1968, the action was concentrated on the Democratic side, as first Eugene McCarthy, and then Robert F. Kennedy (RFK), mounted primary campaigns against the Johnson administration's Vietnam War policy. It produced a drama worthy of Shakespeare.

Both McCarthy and Kennedy were senators; McCarthy from Minnesota, Kennedy from New York. Of the two, Kennedy—the younger brother of the late president—was the heavyweight. But McCarthy entered the race first, attracted a legion of young volunteers with the passion of his cause and the cool, cerebral nature of his candidacy. And he drove Johnson—who had not yet formally entered the race—to the political sidelines with an unexpectedly strong showing in the New Hampshire primary.

In the wake of that political shock wave, Kennedy entered the Democratic race, offering passion, poignancy and a link to the powerful Kennedy legacy. Through the remaining primaries RFK drew vibrant crowds that a rock star would envy, and began to pile up victories as his brother had done eight years earlier.

Kennedy won first in Indiana over McCarthy and the state's favorite son, Gov. Roger Branigin, then again in Nebraska. He broke stride briefly with a close loss to McCarthy in Oregon, before finishing strong with primary victories in South Dakota and California in early June.

With his victory in California, Kennedy was positioned to seriously challenge Humphrey, now the vice president, for the nomination at the Democratic convention in Chicago. Although Humphrey had not competed in any of the primaries, he was in the catbird seat as Johnson's heir apparent and had picked up a large number of delegates in the non-primary states.

But Kennedy had proved his vote-getting ability in the primaries, fashioning a broad-based "have not" coalition of rural, minority, and blue-collar ethnic voters in high-turnout events. In California, Nebraska, and South Dakota, the number of votes cast in the Democratic primary in 1968 surpassed the party's previous high in each state. In Indiana, the turnout for the Democratic presidential primary was the largest in the state's history, before or since.[51]

But the prospect of a dramatic convention showdown with Humphrey ended suddenly the night of the California primary, as Kennedy was shot after addressing a victory party in Los Angeles. He died barely a day later.

His final words to his supporters that night looked toward the future and what was to be one of the most tumultuous and eventful conventions in the nation's history: "So, my thanks to all of you," Kennedy concluded, "and it's on to Chicago and let's win there."[52]

3

Evolution Speeds Up

The Modern Era of Nominating Presidents

The Democratic convention that met in Chicago in August of 1968 was one of the most volatile and historic ever held. It met amid controversy over the long-running war in Vietnam, lingering sorrow from the assassination of Robert Kennedy, and widespread frustration with a Democratic nominating process that left Vice President Hubert Humphrey poised to claim the party's nomination without going before the voters in a single primary state.

Humphrey ultimately prevailed, but at a price. For out of the Chicago convention would come the impetus for a sweeping overhaul of the presidential nominating process that is still being felt to this day.

Through the 1970s and 1980s, the Democrats took the lead, revisiting their nominating rules after each election—sometimes tweaking them, sometimes making wholesale changes, but always making alterations that would make the terrain of the nominating contest a bit different every four years. In the 1990s, though, the Republicans voiced the most agitation with the system—underscoring the reality that a party's interest in reform often increases after presidential election defeats.

In the process, the nominating process has been opened to greater grass-roots participation than ever before, as the number of presidential primaries steadily increased over the last third of the twentieth century to include virtually the entire country. The changes would affect Democrats and Republicans alike, since in most states the primaries that were created applied to both parties.

The shift in decision-making power from the convention to the primaries was felt immediately. No candidate since Humphrey in 1968 has won the nomination of either major party without first competing in the primaries. And no candidate since Democrat George McGovern in 1972 has been nominated without winning the most votes in his party's primaries.

Voter participation in the primaries jumped immediately from barely 12 million in 1968 to more than 22 million in 1972, en route to a total in excess of 30 million in recent elections. Yet the value of increased voter participation would be undercut by the movement of many states to earlier and earlier primary dates, with the result that only voters in the first few states would be guaranteed a meaningful voice in the selection of the Democratic and Republican nominees.

DEMOCRATS CHANGE THE RULES

The Democratic convention in 1968 was highly unusual from the start. It was held in an emotional cauldron, as antiwar protestors battled police in bloody confrontations in downtown Chicago, while several miles away within the convention hall, the tenuous control of the party establishment was constantly being tested.

For the first time since the Republicans' bitter gathering in 1912, the legitimacy of the convention itself was thrown into question. Supporters of Kennedy and Sen. Eugene McCarthy vociferously complained of archaic, anti-democratic state delegate-selection processes that boosted Humphrey, and of ham-handed tactics by party leaders at the convention that maintained Humphrey's delegate majority and their control of the party apparatus.

To mollify the dissidents, a variety of proposals were floated to review the party's nominating rules before the next election. The Humphrey forces and their allies within the Democratic establishment had little interest in such a wholesale rules review. But desperate to unite the party for the fall campaign, they made no effort to actively oppose it.

On the critical roll call, held near midnight of the second day of the convention, the delegates approved a minority report from the convention rules committee that would open the door to the overhaul of the nominating process. The vote: 1,350 for the minority report; 1,206 against. "Many people thought this was the way to throw the liberals a bone," noted veteran Democratic Party activist Anne Wexler, "plus the fact that nobody understood it."[1]

At the time, the vote was hardly seen as a mandate for reform, since it was held amid considerable confusion on the floor. Many delegates apparently thought they were voting merely to ban the unit rule (which required all delegates within a state delegation to support the majority's position) or to limit delegate selection in the future to the year of the convention, both issues of the moment at the 1968 convention. But whether they knew it or not—or at that point even cared—the delegates had also approved the creation of a special commission to review the party's nominating process.

A New Direction

In the wake of Humphrey's narrow defeat that November, two commissions were actually appointed by the incoming Democratic National Committee (DNC) chairman, Fred Harris. One panel, headed by Rep. James O'Hara of Michigan, focused on a review of convention rules; the other, led first by Sen. McGovern of South Dakota (and later by Rep. Donald Fraser of Minnesota), focused on the process of delegate selection, or basically, everything else related to the nominating process.

The McGovern-Fraser commission quickly emerged as the greater catalyst for change. Its 28 members included a trio of future presidential candidates—Sens. McGovern, Harold Hughes of Iowa, and Birch Bayh of Indiana—plus some future stars in the party, such as George Mitchell (then a Democratic national committeeman from Maine who later would be the Senate majority leader) and Warren Christopher (a California lawyer who would later serve as secretary of state in the Clinton administration).

The commission was well stocked with proponents of reform. But it was short on representatives from organized labor and the party's urban machines that could be counted on to defend the status quo. "The commission ran the gamut from 'A' to 'B,' " said Christopher, "not from 'A' to 'Z.' "[2]

The commissioners heard plenty of testimony about how closed the Democratic nominating process had become—from "a district meeting that had been held in the locked basement of a local party leader" to "a precinct caucus that had been convened on a moving bus."[3]

Critics of the commission claimed it was the revenge of the defeated, driven by white, middle-class activists who had backed McCarthy or Kennedy in 1968 and valued the cause of openness in the nominating process more than the health of the Democratic Party.

Yet reformers held the upper hand on the McGovern-Fraser Commission, and their dominance was reflected in its final product, a document titled *Mandate for Reform*. It called on state Democratic organizations to implement 18 guidelines before the 1972 campaign that would in essence shift power in the party's presidential nominating process from the traditional party kingmakers to grass-roots voters.

"Out" went the unit rule where party leaders could control whole delegations, automatic delegate seating for party officials, and any delegate selection before the calendar year of the convention, which had enabled party leaders to establish their hegemony over the process before the field of candidates had even formed.

"In" came the requirement that minorities, women, and youth be reasonably represented in each state delegation—a controversial requirement that was widely regarded as a quota system. Also "in" was a rule tightening the connection between candidates and their delegates, which had the effect of reducing the bloc of uncommitted delegates that in the past had helped keep nominating contests open until the convention.

In their totality, these changes represented a revolutionary reorientation of the nominating process from a laissez faire system that gave wide latitude to the state parties to a highly centralized system where the basic rules were dictated from national party headquarters in Washington. The guidelines were approved by the DNC in early 1971.

Unintended Consequence: A Proliferation of Primaries

Yet from the start, the changes in the nominating process brought unintended consequences. Many members of the McGovern-Fraser Commission hoped their handiwork would encourage many states to elect their delegates in the "town hall" setting of a caucus or convention, which in turn would lead to an openly run national convention where issues could be meaningfully discussed and a nominee chosen in deliberative fashion.

By making caucuses more open and fair, observed Austin Ranney, a political scientist and McGovern-Fraser commission member, the hope was that "participation in them would greatly increase, and consequently the demand for more primaries would fade away. . . . But," he added, "we got a rude shock."[4]

Few commissioners wanted more primaries, viewing this alternative as one that would increase the quantity of voter participation but would likely reduce the quality. Yet many state Democratic officials quickly found the easiest way to comply with the new guidelines was to have their states establish a presidential primary.

Several factors were at play. Caucuses, by their nature, are more closed in their operation than a primary, draw lower turnouts, and are less apt to attract attention from the candidates or the media. In their basic form, they are a series of neighborhood meetings that mainly attract party activists to what is the first step in a multi-stage delegate selection process that often culminates weeks or months later at a state convention.

Even in a famous caucus state such as Iowa, only the first round of voting in the dead of winter draws attention. By the time the delegates are actually selected during the spring, the candidates and the media are long gone.

A primary, in contrast, is comparatively simple in operation and very public in execution. To be sure, primaries come in different forms. Some feature a direct vote for candidates (called a preference vote) that determines the distribution of a state's delegates. In some, there is a preference vote with a separate election of delegates (often called a nonbinding or "beauty contest" primary). And in some instances, there is an election for delegates but no vote for candidates at all.

Yet in every case a primary is like a general election, a daylong vote at hundreds, or even thousands, of polling places around a state. The ease of casting a primary ballot stands in contrast to participation in an often time-consuming caucus. And the results of a primary are usually known immediately.

Many party leaders, as well as students of politics, actually prefer the caucus process. Unlike a primary, which can attract a flood of independent voters and even members of the other party, a caucus is a party-run event that is almost always dominated by the most interested and active party members. It is usually structured to allow time for the discussion of party business, and can prove a fertile recruiting ground for party workers. Yet in the political ethos of the late twentieth century—in which "one man, one vote" has been exalted—greater voter participation, rather than less, has been considered a virtue, tipping the scale toward the creation of more and more presidential primaries.

By early 1972, a half dozen states had created or reinstituted a primary, pushing the total above 20 for the first time ever. This new movement was evident in all parts of the country. Two new primaries were birthed in the Northeast (Maryland and Rhode Island), two in the South (North Carolina and Tennessee), and single primaries were created in the Midwest (Michigan) and the West (New Mexico).

By 1972, most of the nation's most populous states were holding presidential primaries—including the Sun Belt giants of California and Florida, as well as the major Frost Belt behemoths of New York, Pennsylvania, Ohio, Michigan and Illinois. Just as important, the number of Democratic delegates elected in primary states jumped from 40 percent of the convention in 1968 to nearly two-thirds in 1972. And primaries have continued to provide the vast majority of delegates to both parties' conventions ever since.[5]

The growth in presidential primaries quickly changed the whole dynamic of the nominating process. In the convention-oriented system of the previous half century, the few primaries in existence served as a vehicle for candidates to showcase their vote-getting appeal. But primaries then could only advance a candidate's cause. It was at the conventions where the choices were made, and it was the party leaders that had the final say there.

In the post-Chicago politics of the 1970s, though, the primaries not only became the one and only route to the nomination, but the place where nominations were settled. The once powerful party leadership was largely reduced to a spectator's role.

And the role of the conventions they once dominated quickly began to diminish. By the 1970s, conventions had become a venue where front-runners flicked away last ditch challenges. By the mid-1980s, their importance had been reduced even further—to a giant pep rally for the party and its nominee where a coveted consolation prize for defeated candidates was a prime-time speaking slot. That is where things still stand today.

THE 1970S: PRIMARIES DECIDE

The new primary-oriented nominating process was an immediate success at the ballot box (see figure 3.1). Altogether, almost 16 million votes

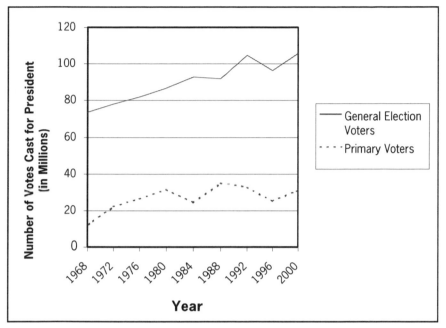

Figure 3.1 The Primary Electorate: Much Smaller Than November

were cast in the Democratic primaries in 1972, plus more than 6 million in the Republican primaries (where President Richard Nixon faced nominal opposition)—a total of 22 million primary votes. That was nearly double the number in any previous year.

Six more primaries were added to the mix in 1976. And with competitive contests in both parties, voter participation jumped again to more than 26 million.

Voter involvement in the caucus states was a bit more difficult to gauge. Over the years, state party officials have often given caucus attendance as estimates rather than exact numbers. Yet it is probably safe to say that several hundred thousand voters at most take part in caucuses each election year, with the caucus turnout never rising above a small fraction of the number that participate in presidential primaries.

Several factors stimulated the dramatic rise in voter participation in the nominating process in the 1970s. Most obvious was the sharp increase in primaries, which for the first time in 1976 included more than half the states. Some, such as Michigan and Wisconsin, held "open" primaries, where any registered voter, not just Democrats or Republicans, could participate in the primary of their choice.

In addition, most nominating contests in the 1970s were highly competitive from the start of the primary season to the finish. The two Democratic nominating battles in the 1970s brought large fields of candidates that spanned the political spectrum. The 1976 Republican race featured the boldest primary challenge to an incumbent president since 1912, as former California Gov. Ronald Reagan mounted a dogged challenge to President Gerald Ford.

With primaries electing more delegates than ever before, candidates were encouraged to compete more broadly for delegates, rather than carefully picking and choosing the contests they entered. Further encouraging Democratic candidates into nationwide campaigning was a decision by party rules-makers after the 1972 election to abolish winner-take-all primaries in favor of proportional representation. Candidates could now gain a share of a state's delegates even if they did not win the state. And with most of the primaries in the 1970s held in May and June, rather than in February and March as is now the case, every vote was meaningful, whether cast in the cold of winter or the warmth of spring (see table 3.1).[6]

Leveling the Playing Field

The democratization of the nominating process made the playing field for the candidates more level than it had ever been. The terrain was noticeably easier for long shot candidates, more difficult for front-runners, as McGovern in 1972 and Jimmy Carter in 1976 won the first two Democratic nominations under the new party rules. Both candidates were consummate long shots, beginning their campaigns in single digits in the public opinion polls.

The mood of the times undoubtedly contributed to the volatility. The debilitating decade-long war in Vietnam ended in the mid-1970s not with victory but disengagement. In August 1974, Nixon had to resign from office in disgrace—the first time in the nation's history that a president had been forced from office. And the economy was in and out of the doldrums, with talk at the end of the decade of a "misery index" to measure just how poorly it was doing. The 1970s were not a good time to be in a position of authority.

In the wake of the Watergate crisis that toppled Nixon, Congress

Table 3.1.   Voter Participation Through the Years: Votes Cast in Presidential Primaries as a Percentage of Votes Cast in Fall General Election

Since the dramatic growth of presidential primaries began in the 1970s, voter participation in the nominating process has increased dramatically. From 1912 through 1968, when the number of primaries was comparatively low, the combined vote in the Democratic and Republican primaries represented barely 15 percent of the fall presidential election vote. Since 1972, that figure has been better than 30 percent. The highest primary turnouts have tended to come in years when both parties have spirited, open contests for their nominations, or an incumbent has a serious challenge for renomination. Still, turnout for the primaries has always been a distinct minority of those who cast ballots in November. The primary and general election vote totals below include the District of Columbia.

	Democrats	Republicans	Primaries	General Election	Primary Turnout as % of General
Convention Era					
1912	12	13	3,236,015	15,043,029	21.5%
1916	20	20	3,111,065	18,535,445	16.8%
1920	16	20	3,757,919	26,768,457	14.0%
1924	14	17	4,289,043	29,099,380	14.7%
1928	16	15	5,374,508	36,801,510	14.6%
1932	16	14	5,299,929	39,747,783	13.3%
1936	14	12	8,501,618	45,656,991	18.6%
1940	13	13	7,696,506	49,817,149	15.4%
1944	14	13	4,139,214	47,976,670	8.6%
1948	14	12	4,805,120	48,691,494	9.9%
1952	16	13	12,729,419	61,550,918	20.7%
1956	19	19	11,660,864	62,026,908	18.8%
1960	16	15	11,224,631	68,838,219	16.3%
1964	16	16	12,182,774	70,644,592	17.2%
1968	15	15	12,008,620	73,211,875	16.4%
Primary Era					
1972	21	20	22,182,246	77,718,554	28.5%
1976	27	26	26,426,777	81,555,889	32.4%
1980	34	34	31,438,276	86,513,813	36.3%
1984	29	25	24,584,868	92,652,842	26.5%
1988	36	36	35,127,051	91,594,809	38.4%
1992	39	38	32,935,932	104,425,014	31.5%
1996	35	42	24,939,013	96,277,223	25.9%
2000	40	43	31,201,862	105,396,627	29.6%
Summary					
Convention Era	(1912–1968)		110,017,245	694,410,420	15.8%
Primary Era	(1972–2000)		228,836,025	736,134,771	31.1%
Total	(1912–2000)		338,853,270	1,430,545,191	23.7%

Source: Adapted from *Congressional Quarterly's Guide to U.S. Elections, Volume I,* 307, 666–88.

passed a new system of campaign financing that further changed the presidential nominating process.

Through 1972, nominating and general election campaigns for president were privately financed, with candidates often turning to a handful of well-heeled "fat cats" to fund their campaigns.

Starting in 1976, there was a taxpayer-supported presidential campaign fund, which completely financed the campaigns of the Democratic and Republican nominees in the general election, and partially financed candidates in the primaries. The system is still in existence.

To become eligible for funding in the primaries, candidates must first raise $5,000 from each of least 20 states, with only $250 of a contribution counting toward the threshold. Once qualified, $250 of each individual contribution to a candidate is matched up to the national spending ceiling, which in 2004 is expected to be in the vicinity of $45 million.

Candidates that accept matching federal funds—and the vast majority have since 1976—must comply with both state-by-state and national spending limits. Candidates, though, also have the option of opting out of the public finance system and spending as much as they like in the primaries. George W. Bush took this alternate fund-raising approach in 2000, and the success of his campaign may encourage other candidates to follow suit in the future. Yet those who do say "no" to public financing still cannot accept individual contributions in excess of $2,000 (raised by Congress in 2002 from the previous limit of $1,000).[7]

A Decade for Dark Horses

The layout of the nominating calendar in the 1970s was tailor made for underdogs such as McGovern and Carter. The primary calendar was arranged like stepping stones, enabling a dark horse candidate to use victory in one state to raise money for the next.

The Iowa caucuses were in January; the New Hampshire primary over a month later. And more than two-thirds of the primaries in 1972 and 1976 were held in May and June, ensuring that the spring primaries—not just those at the beginning of the calendar—would be meaningful.

It is doubtful that McGovern or Carter could have won their party's nomination in the convention system, or for that matter, in the increasingly "front-loaded" primary system that has developed since the

1970s, where success is heavily dependent on having tens of millions of dollars on hand before the primaries begin.

Yet each candidate was well suited for the years in which they ran: McGovern, with a passionate antiwar candidacy when the nation was still engulfed in Vietnam; Carter, with an emphasis on personal ethics in the wake of the Watergate scandal that felled Nixon. "Under the old system, where national convention delegates were mainly chosen by party leaders, I would have had no chance," McGovern said in February 1972 before the first primary was held. "Ed Muskie (the early Democratic front-runner) would have the nomination cinched by now."[8]

McGovern established the model for the modern nominating campaign. He launched his campaign in early 1971, long before any of his Democratic rivals, and was the only significant candidate to take on Muskie in either Iowa or New Hampshire. McGovern correctly figured that he did not have to beat the Maine senator in either state. Merely exceeding the low expectations set for him, McGovern figured, would establish him as a serious contender while weakening Muskie. He was right on both counts.

As the champion of the Democratic left, McGovern had limitations as a vote-getter, even within his own party. He won only eight primaries in 1972—none in the South, none in the industrial states from Pennsylvania west to Illinois. And he drew barely 25 percent of the overall Democratic primary vote, finishing second to Humphrey in the overall tally and barely ahead of Alabama Gov. George Wallace, who was a close third.

But McGovern ran well in a number of high-profile primary states on which the media tended to focus—New Hampshire, Oregon, Wisconsin, Nebraska, and California. In the latter three, the number of ballots cast in the Democratic primary in 1972 was higher than in any year before or since. They were states with a progressive tradition that McGovern was able to tap and a long heritage of presidential primaries that gave their contests currency.

McGovern buttressed his high-profile triumphs with a series of victories that occurred well below the radar screen. His dedicated cadre of supporters was able to dominate action in a number of low-turnout caucus and primary states, such as the one in New York, where at the time, the names of candidates were not listed on the ballot. These were quiet backwaters of the nominating process that the party establishment had dominated in the past. But seemingly hamstrung by the new rules, the party leadership in many of these places either abandoned the field or were outmaneuvered by McGovern, who possessed a knowledge of the party's new nominating rules that none of his rivals could match.

McGovern was poised to win the nomination before the Democratic convention opened that July in Miami Beach. The proceedings underscored the new role of the convention—as a ratifying stage where the winner in the primaries fended off eleventh hour challenges to his nomination.

In an attempt to block McGovern, his opponents sought to strip him of delegates he won in California's winner-take-all primary. They argued that the spirit of the party's new rules required the delegates to be divided proportionately to reflect the primary vote, which was Mc-Govern 44 percent, Humphrey 39 percent. Ultimately, the California Democrats abandoned the winner-take-all primary, but McGovern kept them all at the 1972 convention and was nominated on the first ballot.

McGovern was buried under one of the deepest landslides in American history that fall, carrying just one state (Massachusetts). But his nominating campaign remained highly regarded, and his early-starting candidacy quickly became one to emulate. In the contest for the Democratic presidential nomination in 1976, a trio of candidates, including Carter, formally entered the race by January 1975. By the middle of 1975, three more Democrats had joined the field.

A former one-term governor of Georgia, Carter was every bit the dark horse that McGovern had been, so much so that in December 1974, a Gallup Poll on prospective 1976 Democratic presidential candidates listed 31 names; Carter's was not one of them.[9]

Yet in the months ahead, no one navigated the new nominating process better than the highly focused and indefatigable Carter. The smiling Georgia peanut farmer lacked a ready-made network of support, such as McGovern enjoyed in the anti-war movement. But in the post-Watergate election of 1976, where issues of trust and integrity trumped ideology, Carter's inability to be pigeon-holed as a liberal or a conservative served to his advantage in appealing to broad segments of the party. He ran as the "anti-Nixon;" his campaign mantra: "I'll never tell a lie."[10]

Carter basically replicated McGovern's game plan: Put an initial emphasis on the kick-off events in Iowa and New Hampshire, with the hope of strong showings there that would create the momentum to mount a successful nationwide campaign (see table 3.2).

Table 3.2. Presidential Primaries Since 1972: The Only Route to Nomination

Over the last third of a century, primary voters have replaced delegates as the real coin of the realm in presidential nominating politics. No candidate since Hubert Humphrey in 1968 has won their party's nomination without first entering the primaries, and no candidate since George McGovern in 1972 has been nominated without winning more primary votes than any of his rivals.

In the chart below are the aggregate nationwide Democratic and Republican presidential primary results since 1972, both in terms of the percentage of the overall vote won by major candidates and the number of primary states won by each. In most cases, the totals reflect the outcome of presidential preference primaries, where voters balloted directly for candidates. But in a few primary states where there was no preference vote, the results reflect races for delegates, where their identification with presidential candidates was clearly listed on the ballot.

The total vote below is the number of votes cast for all candidates in the party's primaries that year, including the District of Columbia. The nominee is listed in capital letters. An asterisk (*) indicates an incumbent. All candidates are included who polled at least 20 percent of their party's primary vote. The percentages do not add to 100 because not all candidates are listed.

Election	Total Vote	Candidates	%	Primary States Won
1972 Dems	15,993,965	Hubert Humphrey	26	4
		GEORGE McGOVERN	25	8
		George Wallace	24	5
1972 Reps	6,188,281	RICHARD NIXON*	87	18
1976 Dems	16,052,652	JIMMY CARTER	39	16
1976 Reps	10,374,125	GERALD FORD*	53	16
		Ronald Reagan	46	10
1980 Dems	18,747,825	JIMMY CARTER*	51	23
		Edward Kennedy	37	9
1980 Reps	12,690,451	RONALD REAGAN	61	29
		George Bush	23	4
1984 Dems	18,009,217	WALTER MONDALE	38	10
		Gary Hart	36	16
1984 Reps	6,575,651	RONALD REAGAN*	99	24
1988 Dems	22,961,936	MICHAEL DUKAKIS	43	22
		Jesse Jackson	29	5
1988 Reps	12,165,115	GEORGE BUSH	68	34
1992 Dems	20,239,385	BILL CLINTON	52	30
		Jerry Brown	20	2
1992 Reps	12,696,547	GEORGE BUSH*	72	37
		Pat Buchanan	23	0
1996 Dems	10,947,364	BILL CLINTON*	89	32
1996 Reps	13,991,649	BOB DOLE	59	38
		Pat Buchanan	22	1
2000 Dems	14,045,745	AL GORE	76	39
		Bill Bradley	20	0
2000 Reps	17,156,117	GEORGE W. BUSH	63	35
		John McCain	30	7

Note: The winner of the New York Republican delegate-selection primary in 1996 and 2000 is included in the column, "Primary States Won," but the vote from that contest was not totaled in a way to be readily included in the overall turnout.

Source: Adapted from Rhodes Cook, *Race for the Presidency: Winning the 2000 Nomination,* 144–57; *Congressional Quarterly's Guide to U.S. Elections, Volume I,* 377, 410.

The strategy worked perfectly. Carter scored his initial successes in Iowa and New Hampshire by besting candidates on the left (namely, Rep. Morris Udall of Arizona and Bayh). He knocked out Wallace in March primaries in Florida and North Carolina, and turned back the prime contender from the party's establishment center (Sen. Henry "Scoop" Jackson of Washington) in a late April primary in Pennsylvania. With that, Carter was effectively positioned to win the nomination.

He would lose a series of primaries in May and June to two late-starting candidates, California Gov. Jerry Brown and Sen. Frank Church of Idaho. But their victories merely underscored the wisdom of Carter's early start. Their challenges came too little, too late as Carter continued to pile up delegates, even in defeat.

Yet the appearance of Brown and Church did manage to keep voter interest in the Democratic race alive. Four states that voted in the late spring of 1976 set Democratic primary turnout records that stand to this day. Two of the contests were won by Church—in Oregon and his home state of Idaho. In the other two states, Maryland and Rhode Island, Brown grabbed the headlines.

PRESIDENTS AND PRIMARIES: A COMBUSTIBLE MIX

In many primary states, however, the Republican contest between President Ford and Ronald Reagan drew top billing. Normally, the White House can provide an incumbent with tremendous advantages that a challenger within his party can never match—from the "bully pulpit" that the office commands to control of his party's national organization and many of its state affiliates.

Yet in 1976, the contest between Ford and Reagan was waged on almost even terms from start to finish. As the "unelected" vice president of a disgraced president, Ford was weaker than the typical incumbent. As a former two-term governor of the nation's most populous state, Reagan was stronger than the typical challenger. They were treated by the press essentially as equals and Reagan's success at matching Ford nearly vote-for-vote during the primary season was not viewed as a major accomplishment at the time.[11]

The tone of their contest was set at the start in New Hampshire, where Ford won by barely 1,500 votes out of more than 110,000 cast. But it was a case where perception meant everything. Since New Hampshire was widely seen as a conservative state, where Reagan enjoyed the backing of the governor (Meldrim Thomson) and the largest newspaper (the Manchester *Union Leader*), Ford was viewed as the clear winner and Reagan the clear loser.

Fueled by momentum from his New Hampshire victory, Ford went on to win the next four primaries and seemed on the verge of knocking Reagan out of the race. But in a late March contest in North Carolina, the Californian finally broke into the win column. It was a victory that not only saved Reagan's 1976 presidential bid, but his future political career. And it came by a margin of just 12,571 votes out of almost 200,000 cast.

Throughout the rest of the primary season, the Ford-Reagan contest was nip and tuck. Ford stayed ahead in the delegate count virtually the entire time, but Reagan was close on his heels. Ford won significant victories in Florida, Illinois, and Michigan. Reagan took California and Texas. Ford carried all but three primaries east of the Mississippi River (Georgia, Indiana, and North Carolina). Reagan swept all but one primary to the west of the Mississippi (Oregon).

Ford finally nailed down the nomination long after the primary season ended, aided by the perks, powers and ability to sway delegates that the White House offered.

The Reagan camp made a desperate, last-minute attempt to overcome Ford's advantage at the GOP convention that August in Kansas City, by promoting a proposal that would require candidates to announce their vice-presidential selection before the convention balloting. The Reagan camp was hopeful that any choice that Ford might make would alienate a part of his narrow delegate majority.

For his part, Reagan indicated that his running mate would be Sen. Richard Schweiker of Pennsylvania, a little-known moderate Republican that Reagan aides hoped could pry away delegates from Ford in the Northeast. But the Ford forces beat back the rules challenge on the convention floor and went on to score a first ballot victory. Ultimately, Ford selected Sen. Bob Dole of Kansas as his running mate.

"The fact that the president was the president was the crucial factor in how the race came out," said Ford media consultant John Deardourff. "If it had been Reagan against Ford and Ford had not been president, he would have lost."[12]

In the overall Republican primary vote, Ford's margin over Reagan was just 7 percentage points, 53-to-46 percent. And the tally could have been much closer or even reversed if Reagan had seriously contested major industrial states such as New Jersey, Ohio, and Pennsylvania. There, a lack of funds and a reluctance to challenge the pro-Ford state party organizations resulted in a tepid Reagan effort.

Still, voter turnout for the Ford-Reagan contest topped 10 million votes. It was well below the Democratic primary total in 1976 of 16 million, but represented a new high for the GOP in an era when it was still clearly the minority party (see table 3.3).

THE 1980S: BACK TO THE FUTURE

The 1970s were a unique time in the evolution of the presidential nominating process. The playing field was as level as it has ever been between dark horses and front-runners. The growing number of primaries gave millions of additional voters a role in the process, and with so many primaries held in late spring, nominating contests remained open until the primary season was over. In short, not just the voters in the early states had a say, so did those in states that voted late.

But this period did not last long. No little-known dark horse has gone on to win his party's nomination since the 1970s. The closest parallels—Michael Dukakis in 1988 and Bill Clinton in 1992—had both moved into the top tier of the Democratic field before the primaries began.[13]

The Democratic rules makers played a hand in restoring an advantage to the front-runners. After the 1980 election, party leaders—concerned that the reform rules had gone too far in muting the influence of party and elected officials in the nominating process—created a special category of automatic delegate slots for party and elected officials. Popularly known as "superdelegates," the new positions were reserved for Democratic members of Congress, governors, and members of the Democratic National Committee.

In creating this new class of delegates, party officials had several goals in mind. They wanted to reengage Democratic leaders across the country in the presidential nominating process, add an element of "peer review" that had been missing from the process in the 1970s, and create a firewall to blunt any party outsider that built up a head of steam in the primaries. Superdelegates have comprised roughly 15 to 20 percent of

Table 3.3. Presidents, Renomination, and Reelection

Since the creation of presidential primaries in 1912, every president who actively sought another term won renomination. But not every president subsequently won reelection. The common denominator for incumbent success: A smooth path to renomination. Presidents who ran virtually unopposed within their own party won another term. Presidents who faced significant opposition for renomination ended up losing in the general election.

Only two presidents were beaten for reelection during the long period when conventions decided the nominee (1912–68). But three presidents have been defeated in the shorter span since 1972 in which the primaries have been dominant. The chart below shows the presidents who have sought another term since 1912, their share of their party's primary vote and first-ballot convention delegates (before any shifts), and their ultimate fate in the general election.

A president with an asterisk (*) after his name was completing a full term when he sought reelection. The primary vote for President Lyndon Johnson in 1964 includes the vote cast for favorite sons and uncommitted delegate slates; Johnson was subsequently nominated by acclamation at the Democratic convention.

President George Bush won the same share of the Republican primary vote (72 percent) in 1992 as Franklin D. Roosevelt did on the Democratic side in 1940. FDR's showing, however, came amid speculation that he would not seek a third term, which he ultimately won. Bush drew more focused competition from conservative commentator Pat Buchanan in 1992, and was beaten in the fall.

	Incumbent's Percentage of:		
	Primary Vote	Convention Delegates	General Election Result
Convention Era (1912–68)			
William Howard Taft (1912)*	34%	52%	Lost
Woodrow Wilson (1916)*	99	99.9	Won
Calvin Coolidge (1924)	68	96	Won
Herbert Hoover (1932)*	33	98	Lost
Franklin D. Roosevelt (1936)*	93	100	Won
Franklin D. Roosevelt (1940)*	72	86	Won
Franklin D. Roosevelt (1944)*	71	92	Won
Harry Truman (1948)	64	75	Won
Dwight Eisenhower (1956)*	86	100	Won
Lyndon Johnson (1964)	88	100	Won
Primary Era (1972–present)			
Richard Nixon (1972)*	87	99.9	Won
Gerald Ford (1976)	53	53	Lost
Jimmy Carter (1980)*	51	64	Lost
Ronald Reagan (1984)*	99	99.9	Won
George Bush (1992)*	72	95	Lost
Bill Clinton (1996)*	88	99.7	Won

Source: Adapted from *Congressional Quarterly's Guide to U.S. Elections, Volume I*, 313.

the Democratic convention since 1984 and have often lined up en masse behind the front-runner.[14]

New Trend: The Early Exit

Also during the 1980s, more states began jockeying among themselves for an early spot on the calendar. And as the number of early events grew, more and more candidates began exiting the race after just a few contests.

In 1968, just one state (New Hampshire) held its primary before the end of March. In 1980, there were 10. And in 1988, the number had grown to 22, or more than half of all primaries held. It quickly became the norm for nominations to be decided long before the conclusion of the primary season, with millions of voters in the later-voting states denied a meaningful choice.

The shape of the future was visible on the Republican side in 1980. Off his strong showing against President Ford four years earlier, Reagan was the early front-runner. After a shaky start, he dispatched his field of rivals long before the primary season was over.

George Bush—the erstwhile Houston congressman, Republican National Committee (RNC) chairman, director of the Central Intelligence Administration (CIA), ambassador to China, and later "number 41" in the pantheon of presidents—upset Reagan in the Iowa caucuses.

Yet brandishing what he described as "Big Mo," Bush could not build on his Iowa success as McGovern and Carter had done earlier. He lost badly to Reagan in New Hampshire, dissipating all the momentum he had generated in Iowa.[15]

For a few weeks, Rep. John Anderson of Illinois was a factor in the race. A moderate Republican, who it was said "carried his wallet on the right and wore his heart on the left," nearly won upset victories in Massachusetts and Vermont in early March. But after losing primaries to Reagan in Illinois and Wisconsin, Anderson quit the race in April in favor of an independent presidential bid.[16]

Anderson's meteoric rise during the early Republican primaries drew a flurry of favorable media attention. But his demise underscored the basic nature of the GOP as a "center-right" party, that Reagan's dominance in the primaries showed was moving even further to the right. But Anderson left a legacy of sorts, as his candidacy helped produce record GOP primary turnouts in Illinois and Wisconsin that stand to this day.

Meanwhile, Bush doggedly continued to campaign against Reagan, and with primary victories in Connecticut, Massachusetts, Michigan and Pennsylvania, ran well enough to secure the number two spot on the Republican ticket. But after New Hampshire, he was never again a serious threat to Reagan and withdrew from the race in late May with 12 primaries still to be held.[17]

Nearly 4.4 million of the 12.7 million votes cast in the Republican primaries in 1980 were from those 12 late-voting states, which included California, Ohio, and New Jersey. Put another way, fully one-third of the GOP primary voters in 1980 cast their ballots at a time when Reagan was the only remaining choice. It was a precursor of things to come.

Another President Under Challenge

Like the Republicans in 1976, the Democrats in 1980 had their own brush with political regicide in a contest that featured two flawed political heavyweights.

In one corner was Sen. Edward Kennedy of Massachusetts, the youngest of the Kennedy brothers and champion of the liberal wing of the Democratic Party. He was saddled with "character issues" in the form of a deteriorating marriage and memories of Chappaquiddick (a controversial incident in 1969 in which a young woman had drowned in a car Kennedy was driving).

In the other corner was Carter, now the embattled incumbent, who had never overcome his outsider status to establish a firm base of support within the Democratic Party. Polls taken in the summer of 1979 showed Carter trailing Kennedy as the choice of Democratic voters by a margin of more than 2-to-1.[18]

But the romantic aura that surrounded the presidential campaigns of his older brothers never attached itself to the younger Teddy. And as he formally announced his candidacy in November 1979, a confluence of events quickly gave Carter the upper hand.

First and foremost was the outbreak of the Iran hostage crisis, which created a "rally round the flag" sentiment that benefited the incumbent. Second, but also significant, was Kennedy's obvious lack of preparedness for a national race. It was evident in a television interview with newsman Roger Mudd in which Kennedy had trouble articulating his reasons for seeking the presidency.[19]

Against this backdrop, the Democratic nominating campaign of 1980 played out in two phases. In the first, which encompassed Iowa, New Hampshire and the other early states, Democrats essentially cast a "no" vote on Kennedy. Carter easily won the Iowa caucuses, plus seven of the first eight primaries, losing only Kennedy's home state of Massachusetts. By late March, Carter had built a commanding lead in the delegate count that he would never lose.

With the nomination basically settled, phase two became a referendum on the president and his competence to govern, particularly in the face of a mounting recession. Kennedy became a vehicle for protest for millions of Democrats who wanted to cast a "no" vote on Carter. And he beat the president in nine of the spring primaries.

For the year, turnout for the Democratic primaries increased to nearly 19 million voters, due as much to the continued growth in primaries—approaching 35 in 1980—than the attractive nature of the contest.

In the end, the outcome was not as close as the Ford-Reagan contest four years earlier. Carter defeated Kennedy by the clear-cut margin of 14 percentage points in the overall Democratic primary vote, 51-to-37 percent. But Kennedy carried the cornerstones of the modern-day Democratic presidential coalition, the major states of the industrial Northeast (New York, Pennsylvania, New Jersey and Massachusetts) as well as California.

And down in the weeds was an additional sign of problems for the Democratic Party—a visible distaste by more than 1 million primary voters with the choice they were offered. They cast their primary ballots neither for Carter or Kennedy, but for some variation of "None of the above." In no other election before or since has that total been so high.

The Democratic convention in New York in August served as a "last hurrah" for what had once been the decisive event of the presidential nominating process. In a desperate bid to deny Carter the nomination, the Kennedy forces mounted an attack on a party rule binding delegates to the candidate they were elected to support. With a commanding majority of the delegates, Carter would be easily nominated if the rule was enforced. If the rule was overturned and delegates could vote for whom they pleased, regardless of state law or previous commitments, the situation was uncertain.

When the issue came to a vote, the Carter side prevailed, nailing down the nomination in the process. Yet little did anyone know at the time, this skirmish marked the end of competitive conventions in any form. Beginning in 1984, they would become made for TV events, totally designed to appeal to voters outside the convention hall.

As for the "binding" rule, Democrats dropped it after the 1980 election. As for Carter, he lost badly to Reagan in the fall.

Institutional Power Prevails

Democratic leaders approached 1984 looking for a party insider who could win, and lined up en masse behind former Vice President Walter Mondale. He entered the primaries that year with more institutional advantages than any Democratic candidate since Humphrey in 1968.

As a long-established figure in the party, Mondale drew pre-primary endorsements from a variety of prominent Democratic-oriented interest groups, including the AFL-CIO; held the inside track to win the bulk of the superdelegates; and faced a delegate-selection calendar that for the first time since 1968 featured an increase in party-run caucuses and a decline in primaries (in part due to state budget cuts forced by a recession in the early 1980s).

Yet with all these advantages, Mondale still proved highly vulnerable. The wealth of institutional support left him vulnerable to an insurgent challenge from Colorado Sen. Gary Hart, who had effectively managed McGovern's long shot candidacy for the Democratic nomination 12 years earlier.

And Mondale's expected appeal to black primary voters was muted by the candidacy of the Rev. Jesse Jackson, a colleague of the late Martin Luther King. Jackson won only one primary in 1984, in Louisiana. But he took a large majority of the black vote in the South and urban centers of the industrial Frost Belt.

Jackson's candidacy helped Hart, who like McGovern earlier, focused on making a strong showing in the early states. Hart succeeded, with a second-place showing in Iowa that put him in contention in New Hampshire. There, an upset victory by Hart produced two weeks worth of momentum that left Mondale on the brink of elimination.

Hart ran as a "new Democrat," and showed an appeal to independent voters that Mondale could not match. Yet it quickly became evident that the 1980s were not as conducive to dark horse candidacies as the

1970s. Mondale effectively counterattacked. He challenged Hart's credentials for national leadership with the legendary line, "Where's the beef ?"—a takeoff on a popular Wendy's hamburger commercial at the time.

Hart's momentum blunted, Mondale marshaled support among the new group of superdelegates, and scored a succession of primary victories in old-line "machine" states, such as Illinois, New York, and Pennsylvania, where the union vote was large.[20]

But Mondale could not shake Hart, who ran well where the Democratic Party organization and its institutional allies were comparatively weak. Hart carried every primary in New England and every one west of the Mississippi River, including California. At the end of the primary season, the count stood 16 for Hart, 10 for Mondale.

The former vice president never demonstrated much vote-getting appeal during the primaries. He carried just one (West Virginia) with a majority of the vote. And he finished barely ahead of Hart in the overall Democratic primary vote, 38-to-36 percent, with 18 percent for Jackson. It was the most mediocre primary showing by a Democratic nominee since McGovern.

The Democratic primaries of 1984, however, did succeed in engaging voters. Even though the number of primaries had declined, fully 18 million voters cast ballots, only slightly below the Democratic total in 1980. All-time highs for the party were reached in such disparate states as Georgia, North Carolina, Vermont, Illinois, Ohio, New Jersey, and Pennsylvania.

To be sure, the high primary turnout was due in part to the absence of competition on the Republican side, where Reagan ran unopposed for renomination. But it was also a tribute to the competitive nature of the Democratic contest—the last to this day to be unresolved on the final day of the primary season. And it was a tribute to the diverse nature of the Democratic field, each with their appeal to various parts of the Democratic electorate.

Jackson dominated the large turnout of blacks, which was estimated to reach 3 million in the Democratic primaries. Mondale ran well among older voters (at least 60 years old), another high-turnout constituency. Hart dominated among independents, who cast nearly 3.5 million votes in the Democratic primaries.[21]

Still, the outcome of the 1984 presidential race underscored the fact that high primary turnouts in the spring do not always foretell a party's success in the fall (see table 3.4). Mondale's candidacy ended under a 49-state landslide that November, just as McGovern's campaign had a dozen years earlier.

The South Rises Again

By the late 1980s, it was clear that the calendar of primaries and caucuses was dramatically changing in a way that would profoundly affect both candidates and voters alike. The 1984 campaign had provided only a temporary pause in the steady growth of presidential primaries.

In 1988, there were not only more primaries than ever but also a growing array of earlier ones. With Reagan retiring and open nominating contests in both parties, many states figured that a date on the calendar as close as possible to the kickoff events in Iowa and New Hampshire was the likeliest way to exert influence on the nominating process.

But there was not a helter-skelter scramble to the front of the calendar. In a new wrinkle, states within the same region began looking at the possibility of holding their primaries on the same day, the better to draw the attention of the candidates and build voter interest. The regional groupings also had the salutary effect of adding some coherence to a primary calendar that was becoming increasingly crowded and geographically far-flung.

One-day regional groupings of presidential primaries had popped up from time to time in all parts of the country over the previous decade or so. But nowhere was it tried on a grander scale than in the South in 1988.

The centerpiece of the Southern event was Florida, which in 1972 moved its primary date forward from late May to the second Tuesday in March. In 1980, Alabama and Georgia joined Florida, the first incarnation of the event that would become known as "Super Tuesday." In 1984, six other states from New England to Hawaii scheduled their contests on the second Tuesday in March, giving it a national flavor. But it was in 1988 that Super Tuesday reached its apex, with virtually the entire South comprising its cornerstone.

The push for an early Southern primary came from Democratic state legislators across the region, exasperated with a presidential selection process that had produced a number of liberal Democratic nominees with little appeal in the region. Southern Democrats also wanted to draw attention to regional issues, to lure back conservative white voters

Table 3.4.   Big Years for Primary Turnout at the State Level

In terms of primary turnout, 2000 was a banner year for Republicans. Not only did a party-record 17 million voters participate in the GOP primaries, but turnout records (in terms of number of ballots cast) were set in 19 states. For the Democrats, their best year turnout-wise was 1988, when participation peaked at 23 million votes and party turnout records were set in 11 states.

Spirited competition and an open nominating contest (without an incumbent running) have been key factors in producing the strongest primary turnouts. The 2000 Republican contest featured the duel between George W. Bush and John McCain. The 1988 Democratic contest offered Michael Dukakis, Jesse Jackson, Al Gore and Richard Gephardt, each with a foothold in the Democratic electorate that gave their candidacy plausibility.

In the chart below, an asterisk (*) designates an incumbent; a dash (—) indicates the incumbent had no significant opposition for renomination. Given their importance, the Iowa caucuses are included in this table with the primary states. All states have held presidential primaries at one time or another except Alaska, Hawaii, and Wyoming, and Alaska held a primary in 1956 while a territory. Four states established Democratic primary turnout records prior to 1972—Indiana (1968), West Virginia (1960), Minnesota (1956) and North Dakota (1932), as did seven states on the Republican side—Illinois, Minnesota, Nebraska, New Jersey, and South Dakota (all in 1952), plus West Virginia (1928) and North Dakota (1924).

REPUBLICANS

Year	Nominee	Leading Contender	Record Turnouts for GOP	States
2000	G.W. Bush	McCain	19	CA, GA, ID, ME, MD, MA, MI, MO, NH, NY, NC, OH, RI, SC, TX, UT, VT, VA, WA
1996	Dole	Buchanan	8	AZ, CO, DE, MT, NV, OK, OR, TN
1992	G. Bush*	Buchanan	0	
1988	G. Bush	Dole	7	AL, AR, FL, IA, LA, MS, NM
1984	Reagan*	—	0	
1980	Reagan	G. Bush	4	CT, KS, PA, WI
1976	Ford*	Reagan	2	IN, KY
1972	Nixon*	—	0	

DEMOCRATS

Year	Nominee	Leading Contender	Record Turnouts for Democrats	States
2000	Gore	Bradley	5	AZ, DE, ME, UT, WA
1996	Clinton*	—	0	
1992	Clinton	Brown	7	AL, AR, CO, KY, NH, OK, SC
1988	Dukakis	J. Jackson	11	CT, IA, LA, MS, MO, NM, NY, SD, TN, TX, VA
1984	Mondale	Hart	7	GA, IL, NJ, NC, OH, PA, VT
1980	Carter*	E. Kennedy	3	KS, MA, MT
1976	Carter	Udall	6	FL, ID, MD, NV, OR, RI
1972	McGovern	Humphrey	4	CA, MI, NE, WI

Source: Adapted from *America Votes 24,* 42–45; *Race for the Presidency 2000,* 22–138; *Springboard to the White House,* 278–305.

who had abandoned the party, and to create an event so huge and so early in the nominating process (just three weeks after New Hampshire) that it would overshadow all that preceded it.

"We're excited that we can have more impact on presidential . . . nominations than [at] any time since the War of Northern Aggression," explained Mississippi state Rep. Charlie Capps. "Our Confederate money is about to be worth a whole lot more."[22]

Every Southern state signed on to the Super Tuesday event in 1988, with the exception of South Carolina. Maintaining their role as the "New Hampshire of the South," South Carolina Republicans scheduled their primary for the Saturday before Super Tuesday, while the state's Democrats held caucuses on the Saturday after.

But 10 of the 11 states of the old Confederacy voted on Super Tuesday, as did Kentucky and Oklahoma (which are often included in an expansive definition of the region preferred by the author), plus Maryland and Missouri, which border the South. Six other states from Massachusetts to Hawaii also held contests on March 8, 1988, but Super Tuesday that year was clearly the South's day to shine (see table 3.5).

The event was reasonably successful at the ballot box. Nearly 8 million voters across the 13-state version of the South participated in the Democratic primaries, while an additional 4 million voters turned out for the Republican primaries. Fully one out of every three primary ballots cast in the entire 1988 primary season were from that single day in the South.

The results underscored the disparate nature of the Democratic and Republican primary electorates in the late twentieth century South, which in turn was a reasonable microcosm of each party nationally. The GOP universe was smaller than its Democratic counterpart. But predominantly conservative and almost exclusively white, the Republican primary vote was much more ideologically and racially homogenous and more apt to unite behind the front-runner.

In this environment, Vice President George Bush succeeded on a grand scale by clinging tightly to the coattails of the retiring Reagan, whose presidency, a CBS News/New York Times exit poll showed, was viewed positively by almost 90 percent of Southern Republican primary voters. Bush faced a crowded GOP field that included Bob Dole, former Rep. Jack Kemp of New York, and televangelist Pat Robertson, but Bush swept every Southern primary and finished Super Tuesday poised to nail down the GOP nomination.[23]

Table 3.5.   The Southern Regional Primary at Its Apex: March 8, 1988

No region of the country has come closer to holding a one-day primary than the South did on March 8, 1988. The centerpiece of a coast-to-coast votefest that involved nearly 20 states, the rare event involved 10 of the 11 states of the old Confederacy, plus Kentucky and Oklahoma, which are included in some expansive definitions of the South. Republicans in the other Southern state, South Carolina, held a primary on March 5. South Carolina Democrats held caucuses a week later.

Nearly 12 million votes were cast in the Southern primaries March 8, more than one-third of the 35 million primary ballots cast nationwide in 1988. Reflecting the Democratic heritage of the region, roughly two out of every three ballots were cast in the Democratic primaries, and the Democratic turnout exceeded the Republican turnout in every Southern state that voted that day.

Yet the Republican primaries proved more decisive. Beginning with a pivotal win in South Carolina, George Bush swept all the Southern primaries on the GOP side, building a commanding lead in the delegate count that led to his early nomination. The result on the Democratic side, though, was a split decision, a disappointment to many Democratic leaders in the region who had championed the Southern primary idea and hoped it would further the presidential ambitions of one of their own.

Instead, no single Democratic candidate dominated the regional vote, as civil rights activist Jesse Jackson swept the Deep South (with its large black population), Massachusetts Gov. Michael Dukakis won the populous peripheral states of Florida and Texas, and Tennessee Sen. Al Gore won the Mid-South states from North Carolina west to Oklahoma. Dukakis eventually won the Democratic nomination later that spring in primary contests against Jackson and Gore in the industrial Frost Belt, but failed to carry a single Southern state that fall.

No region before or since has tried to group themselves en masse to influence the nominating process. An asterisk (*) indicates that the number of votes cast in the 1988 primary is the party's all-time high in that state.

	Primary Turnouts		Primary Winners	
	Democrats	Republicans	Democrats	Republicans
Alabama	405,642	213,561*	Jackson	Bush
Arkansas	497,544	68,305*	Gore	Bush
Florida	1,273,298	901,222*	Dukakis	Bush
Georgia	622,752	400,928	Jackson	Bush
Kentucky	318,721	121,402	Gore	Bush
Louisiana	624,450*	144,781*	Jackson	Bush
Mississippi	359,417*	158,526*	Jackson	Bush
North Carolina	679,958	273,801	Gore	Bush
Oklahoma	392,727	208,938	Gore	Bush
Tennessee	576,314*	254,252	Gore	Bush
Texas	1,767,045*	1,014,956	Dukakis	Bush
Virginia	364,899*	234,142	Jackson	Bush
TOTAL	7,882,767	3,994,814	—	—

Source: America Votes 18, 48–49.

The Democrats, though, had a result that reflected their larger but more diverse electorate, which gave voice to not one version of the South, but three (see figure 3.2).

Jesse Jackson, making his second bid for the Democratic nomination, was the favorite of the black South. He carried the five states with the highest proportion of black voters casting Democratic primary ballots—Alabama, Georgia, Louisiana, and Mississippi across the Deep South, plus Virginia.

Massachusetts Gov. Michael Dukakis carried populous Florida and Texas on the fringes of the region, where the in-migration from outside the region was large and the Hispanic population, which Dukakis assiduously cultivated, was sizable.

Sen. Al Gore of Tennessee (the son of the 1956 Democratic vice-presidential aspirant) won interior Dixie, from North Carolina west to Oklahoma, where the number of moderate to conservative white voters casting Democratic primary ballots was significant.[24]

With these various parts of the South basically canceling each other out, the Democratic nomination was decided later in Dukakis' favor in the industrial states of the North. That November, like McGovern and Mondale before him, Dukakis failed to carry a single Southern state and was beaten decisively.

As in 1972, 1980, and 1984 before, 1988 was another year for the Democrats where their nominee lost in November after the battle for the party's nomination had produced a strong primary turnout. Almost 23 million ballots were cast in the 36 Democratic primaries, a record for either party, and in 11 states the Democratic turnout reached all-time highs that still stand. Five of the states were in the South, but the number also included New York and the caucus state of Iowa.

Meanwhile, in the more one-sided Republican contest, the primary turnout surpassed 12 million—the second-highest total in party history to that point. The GOP set records in 1988 for ballots cast in seven states, including five in the South and Iowa.

Voter participation in both parties' primaries topped 35 million, which represented 38 percent of the number of votes cast in the presidential election that fall—record highs on both counts.

Yet it was also becoming increasingly clear that many voters no longer had a meaningful voice in the process. For all practical purposes, the Republican contest was over in late March, when Dole quit the race. At the time, a total of 15 primaries remained.

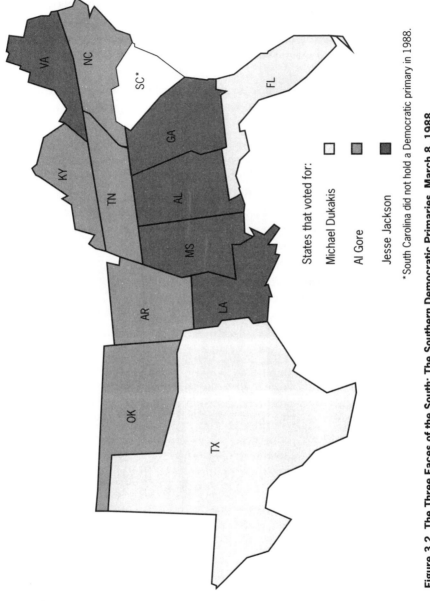

States that voted for:

☐ Michael Dukakis

▨ Al Gore

■ Jesse Jackson

* South Carolina did not hold a Democratic primary in 1988.

Figure 3.2 The Three Faces of the South: The Southern Democratic Primaries, March 8, 1988

The Democratic contest went into cruise control several weeks later, when Dukakis scored a decisive victory in New York that drove Gore from the race. Running one-on-one against Jackson in the remaining 13 primaries, Dukakis easily won all but one, that in the District of Columbia.

Still, in his two bids for the Democratic nomination, Jackson polled nearly 10 million primary votes. In the process, he called attention to himself and the concerns of his black constituency, the most loyal within the Democratic Party.

Pat Robertson's candidacy on the Republican side had a similar effect. The conservative Christian commentator drew more than 1 million votes in his single run for president in 1988. Bush successfully competed against Robertson for votes of the Christian Right, but Robertson's mere presence in the Republican field underscored the growing influence of this constituency within the GOP.

Together, the candidacies of the two ministers demonstrated the ability of political outsiders—with access to powerful constituencies—to affect modern nominating contests, if not actually win them.

THE 1990S: EXPECTING THE UNEXPECTED

Many Democrats had expected to win the White House in 1988; few thought they would do so in 1992. President Bush's high standing in the wake of Allied victory in the Persian Gulf War the previous year had deterred big name Democrats from running against him. Jackson did not run, nor did political heavyweights such as New York Gov. Mario Cuomo. The field that formed was considered to be a weak one.

Candidates still faced a "front-loaded" primary calendar in 1992. But the Super Tuesday Southern event was about half the size that it was in 1988. Georgia moved its primary up a week to the first Tuesday in March. South Carolina, which held a Republican primary in 1988 on the Saturday before Super Tuesday, did so again in 1992 with the Democrats joining in. Alabama, Kentucky and North Carolina dropped back to their traditional state primary dates in the spring. And Virginia abandoned its primary altogether in favor of the caucus process.

Yet even in its truncated form, the Super Tuesday South was able to advance a native son in 1992 in a way that it had failed to do in 1988. The beneficiary was Arkansas Gov. Bill Clinton, who pulled together the disparate strains of the Southern Democratic coalition as none of the party's candidates had been able to do in 1988.

The Comeback Kid

Clinton stumbled as the primary season began, hit by charges of draft evasion during the Vietnam War era and infidelity in his marriage. He limited much of the damage with a contrite appearance on a special edition of CBS' "Sixty Minutes" with wife Hillary, and declared himself the "comeback kid" by finishing second to former Massachusetts Sen. Paul Tsongas in New Hampshire. But of the first five primaries, Clinton could win only one, in Georgia.[25]

Yet that one victory proved a harbinger of things to come, as in the next week, Clinton won South Carolina and the six Southern primaries that remained a part of Super Tuesday. The Southern sweep more than offset Tsongas' victories the same day in his New England backyard (Massachusetts and Rhode Island). And with momentum, Clinton lost only one contested primary the rest of the way—in Connecticut, to former California Gov. Jerry Brown.

Clinton showed himself to be a formidable vote-getter. More than 20 million votes were cast in the Democratic primaries in 1992—second only to the 1988 total. And more than 10 million of the ballots went to Clinton, the highest presidential primary tally for any candidate of either party before 2000.

Meanwhile, Bush's performance on the Republican side underscored the adage that presidents who face dogged opposition for renomination usually lose their bid for reelection. By the time the 1992 primary season opened, the glow of the Gulf War victory had worn off, replaced by concerns about a weakening economy and anger among conservatives with Bush's recanting of his 1988 "no new taxes" pledge.

Bush drew a frisky challenge from conservative commentator Pat Buchanan, who mockingly likened the president to Britain's aloof "King George" of Revolutionary War times, and barnstormed in a bus dubbed "Asphalt One."[26]

While Bush was not as seriously threatened in the primaries as Presidents Ford and Carter had been, Buchanan exposed Bush's problems within his Republican base. The challenger pulled more than 35 percent of the Republican primary vote in New Hampshire and Georgia. And by the end of the primary season, nearly 3 million of the 12.7 million GOP primary ballots had gone to Buchanan. It represented an un-usually large protest vote against a sitting president, particularly within the Republican primaries, where respect for an incumbent usually runs high.

By the end of the 1992 primary season, though, the focus was not on Bush, Buchanan or Clinton, but the budding independent candidacy of wealthy Texas businessman Ross Perot. In Washington state in mid-May, he drew headlines by taking nearly 20 percent of the vote in *both* the Democratic and Republican primaries on write-ins. In North Dakota in June, Perot won the Democratic contest with nearly 10,000 write-in votes, twice as many as Clinton received.

Perot's showings in these late primaries did not win him any dele-gates, but it did illustrate a degree of voter frustration with a nominating process that had determined the winners long before all the states were heard from (see table 3.6).[27]

Bite-sized Regions

Over the last decade or so, the prime criticism of the nominating process has been that it has become too "front-loaded"—with more and more states voting earlier and earlier in the election year. It has produced a system where only the best known, best funded, and best networked candidates stand a chance to win, where only voters in the earliest states have a meaningful say, and where the outcome is determined just when many Americans are beginning to tune into what is happening.

In an attempt to bring a sense of order to the nominating process, many early-voting states in 1996 voluntarily aligned themselves into small regional groupings. Rather than the huge Super Tuesday vote that the South anchored in 1988, there were more bite-sized alignments.

After New Hampshire held its primary on the third Tuesday in Feb-ruary, Arizona and the Dakotas voted a week later, followed by South Carolina on the first Saturday in March.

Then, on the first Tuesday in March came the "Yankee primary," an eight-state vote that included all five New England states outside New Hampshire. The second Tuesday in March featured six primaries in the South, followed a week later by "Big Ten Tuesday," a quartet of contests in the heart of the industrial Midwest. And on the fourth Tuesday in March was a three-state Pacific West primary, dominated by California.

On paper, it appeared to be a fairly rational attempt to bring some

Table 3.6.   A Rise in Third Parties: The Product of a Flawed Nominating Process?

Some of the nation's strongest third-party movements have come in years when one of the major parties has had trouble handling dissent within its nominating process. A baker's dozen worth of third-party and independent candidates have drawn at least 5 percent of the popular vote for president. Four of them came in just two elections—1860 and 1912—when a pair of third-party candidates broke the 5 percent threshold each time.

The Democrats broke asunder on the eve of the Civil War, as did the Republicans in 1912 after the bitter Taft-Roosevelt fight. And in 1968, the third-party candidacy of George Wallace was fueled in part by fissures within the Democratic Party over civil rights that the convention that year in Chicago could not heal, even with its calls for reform of the nominating process.

From the end of the Roaring Twenties through Vietnam and Watergate in the 1970s, Wallace was the only third-party candidate to surpass 5 percent. Yet that threshold has been surpassed three times since 1980—the year that the major party nominations began to be settled before the end of the primary season and millions of primary voters became meaningless bystanders.

In 1980, Rep. John Anderson of Illinois actually began the year as a candidate for the Republican presidential nomination. But after some "close but no cigar" finishes in primaries in New England and his native Midwest, Anderson shifted his sights to an independent presidential bid that ended up drawing nearly 7 percent of the vote. Wealthy businessman Ross Perot won 19 percent of the vote in 1992 running as an independent. Four years later, Perot pulled 8 percent as the nominee of the Reform Party. In the chart below, the 13 third-party efforts that surpassed 5 percent are grouped chronologically according to three basic periods of the nominating process.

The first six of these candidacies occurred during the span of 20 elections that comprised the "Convention Era." Four more took place during the period of 15 elections when there were "Conventions with Primaries." And three have occurred in the shorter eight-election "Primary-Oriented Era" that began in 1972. The latter trio does not include Green Party nominee Ralph Nader, who drew 2.7 percent of the popular vote in 2000, an election which was decided by a much smaller margin than that.

Candidate	Party	Year	% of Vote
Convention Era (1832–1908)			
William Wirt	Anti-Masonic	1832	7.8%
Martin Van Buren	Free Soil	1848	10.1%
Millard Fillmore	Whig-American	1856	21.5%
John Breckinridge	Southern Democrat	1860	18.1%
John Bell	Constitutional Union	1860	12.6%
James Weaver	Populist	1892	8.5%
Conventions with Primaries (1912–68)			
Theodore Roosevelt	Progressive	1912	27.4%
Eugene Debs	Socialist	1912	6.0%
Robert La Follette	Progressive	1924	16.6%
George Wallace	American Independent	1968	13.5%
Primary-Oriented Era (1972–present)			
John Anderson	Independent	1980	6.6%
Ross Perot	Independent	1992	18.9%
Ross Perot	Reform	1996	8.4%

Source: Adapted from *Congressional Quarterly's Guide to U.S. Elections, Volume 1,* 425.

coherence to the glut of early primaries, with the nominating contest in March set to follow a logical geographical progression across the country from New England to the Far West. In practice, though, competition waned by early March, leaving little reason for voters to go to the polls. Democrats did not have a contest at all, since President Clinton was essentially unopposed for renomination, while the Republican race was basically over before it left the Northeast.

Like other front-runners before and since, Senate Majority Leader Bob Dole got off to a shaky start in the GOP contest. He narrowly won the Iowa caucuses, lost New Hampshire to Pat Buchanan, and Delaware and Arizona within the next week to wealthy publisher Steve Forbes. But beginning with a sweep of the Dakotas in late February, Dole was unbeatable, and a succession of primary victories began to quickly accumulate. Even though California had moved its primary up from June to late March, it still voted too late to make a difference.

Dole's early knockout, though, did his candidacy little good. With no competition in the spring primaries and his publicly funded campaign chest virtually exhausted, Dole dropped out of the news. In June, he took the radical step of resigning as Senate majority leader in a bid to jump start his campaign. But he was never able to overcome the long early lead that Clinton had established.[28]

Voter interest in the primaries waned quickly after the decisive early contests in 1996. Even though the number of primaries had increased since 1992 to more than 40, only 25 million voters cast ballots in the 1996 primaries, the majority on the Republican side for the first time since 1952.

And with little campaign activity worthy of note between March and the conventions in August, voter disengagement remained a problem throughout the year. In November, less than a majority of the nation's voting-age population cast ballots, the lowest rate for a presidential election since the electorate was expanded to include women in the 1920s.[29]

Republicans Become Reformers

When Republicans were regularly winning the White House during the 1970s and 1980s, they took a laissez faire attitude toward the nominating process, letting the Democrats worry about its proper construct. But once the GOP began to lose presidential elections in the 1990s, it was the Republicans that led the chorus of critics of the "front-loaded" primary system.

Even before Dole was formally nominated in 1996, the Republican National Committee set up a task force to look at ways to remedy the situation. At their convention in San Diego that summer, Republicans made a first crack at breaking the log jam of early primaries by passing a rule that offered additional delegates in 2000 to states that held their primary or caucus in the spring. But with most states figuring that the attention of an early contest outweighed a few more delegates, the offer of bonus delegates drew few takers.[30]

What took place in 2000 was more of the same—a glut of early primaries. What was different was that something akin to a nationwide primary, or at least a "national sampler," developed on the first Tuesday in March (March 7). Eleven states—including California, New York, and Ohio—scheduled their primaries that day—the cornerstone of a de facto national vote that encompassed states with nearly 40 percent of the population. The event was known as "Titanic Tuesday" to some, "Super Tuesday" to others, although the original Southern-oriented vote of the same name remained on the second Tuesday in March.

Political pundits predicted that the huge mass of early events in 2000 would result in both parties' nominations being settled by the ides of March. And they were right. The Democratic and Republican front-runners, Vice President Al Gore and Texas Gov. George W. Bush, respectively, both scored early knockouts, though Bush's path to victory was much tougher than Gore's.

Arizona Sen. John McCain—a former prisoner-of-war in Vietnam, as well as a party maverick with media appeal—quickly emerged from the crowded GOP field to challenge Bush. Across the month of February, the two traded primary victories. Criss-crossing New Hampshire in his campaign bus, "The Straight Talk Express," McCain scored an upset victory in the Granite State. Bush bounced back with primary wins in Delaware and South Carolina. McCain won in Arizona and Michigan. Bush rebounded with primary triumphs in Virginia and Washington.[31]

Virtually everywhere, Republican primary turnout records were shattered. In New Hampshire, 238,206 ballots were cast, almost 30,000 more than 1996. In South Carolina, the turnout was 573,101, more than double the total of four years earlier. In Michigan, 1,276,770 voted in the McCain-Bush contest, more than 200,000 greater than the previous GOP high in 1976 when Ford was defending his home state.

To the surprise of many, McCain matched Bush, the son of the former president, virtually ballot for ballot through the first month of the primary season. Bush had four primary victories, McCain three. And the aggregate vote count from the first seven Republican primaries was a virtual dead heat: 1,692,999 for Bush, 1,690,310 for McCain—a Bush plurality of less than 3,000 votes out of more than 3 million cast.

No Place for Insurgents

But through February, primaries were held in only one or two states at a time. Once the calendar flipped to March, Bush's superior organization and funding placed him in position to dominate the vast multi-front action on March 7. McCain continued to run well in New England that day. But Bush won everywhere else—New York and Maryland in the Northeast, Georgia in the South, the bellwether states of Ohio and Missouri in the Midwest, and the nation-state of California in the West.

Altogether, Bush took 57 percent of the Republican primary ballots cast on Super Tuesday to McCain's 38 percent, and rolled up a plurality of nearly 1.3 million votes. Without a major victory to point to March 7 and Bush's home region, the South, coming up the following Tuesday, McCain quit the race (see figures 3.3 and 3.4).

Bush had won by mobilizing the Republican core vote. But most of the early primaries were in states that allowed non-Republicans to participate, enabling McCain to mount an effective challenge by attracting the votes of independents and Democrats. In the end, they were not enough to overtake Bush. But they did help produce record Republican turnouts in 15 of the 18 primary states where the two candidates went head-to-head. By the end of the primary season, a record 17 million votes were cast in the Republican primaries, 3 million more than on the Democratic side.

One factor that aided McCain in appealing to non-Republican voters during February was the absence of competing Democratic contests. Since 1980, Democratic rules had protected the leadoff positions for Iowa and New Hampshire by prohibiting other states from voting before early March. That meant that after the New Hampshire primary in early February, the Democratic race essentially went "dark" until the huge cross-country vote on March 7.[32]

The long intermission also meant that the Democratic contest be-

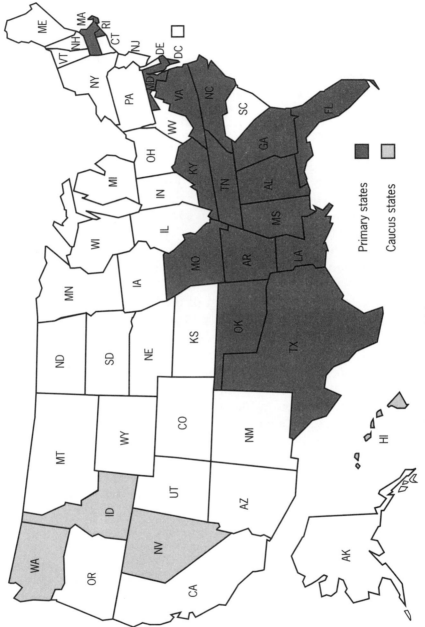

Figure 3.3 The Evolution of Super Tuesday— March 8, 1988

Primary states

Caucus states

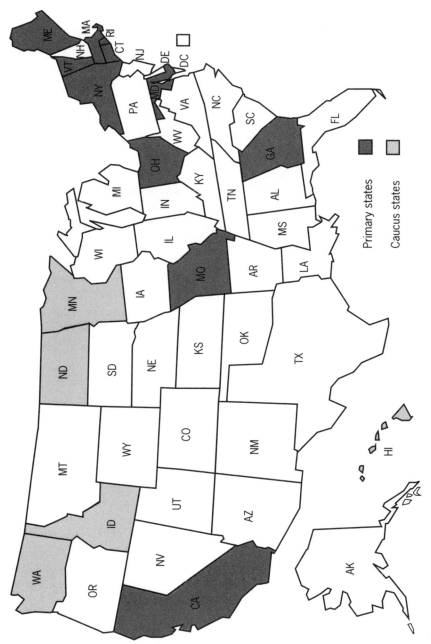

Figure 3.4 The Evolution of Super Tuesday—March 7, 2000

Primary states

Caucus states

tween Gore and former New Jersey Sen. Bill Bradley was overshadowed by the lively Republican road show. Bradley had kept pace with Gore in raising money and drawing media attention in the long period before the primaries. But once the balloting began, Bradley never hit his stride. The vice president won the late January caucuses in Iowa decisively, and the New Hampshire primary narrowly.

The New Hampshire result provided the greatest "what if" of the 2000 nominating season. If a portion of the independents backing McCain had instead voted in the Democratic primary for Bradley, he might have been able to overcome Gore's 6,395-vote margin of victory while McCain, with more than 40,000 votes to spare, would still have won easily on the Republican side.

A Bradley victory in New Hampshire could have changed the dynamic of the Democratic race, at the least providing the former professional basketball star with some momentum going into March 7. As it was, Bradley was 0-for-2 after New Hampshire, and was swept by Gore in all the Democratic contests on Super Tuesday. Bradley quit the race March 9, the same day that McCain pulled the plug on his campaign.

Even though less than half the states had voted by then, both the Democratic and Republican races were over. Cut out of a meaningful role in deciding the 2000 nominees were voters in Florida, Illinois, New Jersey, North Carolina, Pennsylvania, Wisconsin, and more than a dozen other states that held their primaries after the nominations had been decided.

FORWARD, MARCH!

Yet even as the primaries in 2000 were winding down, a new Republican task force was fashioning a proposal for a dramatic overhaul of the nominating process for 2004. The commission, headed by former Tennessee senator and RNC Chairman Bill Brock, recommended that the whole primary calendar be revamped, so that small states would vote first and large states would vote last. That way, the reasoning went, primaries would be spread out from March to June and more voters would be given a meaningful voice, as it would be mathematically impossible for a candidate to acquire a majority of delegates before most, if not all of the states had voted.

The idea, called the "Delaware Plan" because of its state of origin, was not embraced with open arms by the larger states, which feared a loss of influence if they were relegated to the end of the primary season. Still, the plan was approved by a pre-convention meeting of the RNC in the summer of 2000, before being sacrificed on the altar of party harmony before it could reach the floor for a vote.[33]

Meanwhile, the original reformers of the nominating process, the Democrats, have become the party of the status quo. Their lone rules change of note in recent years came at the party's national committee meeting in early 2002, when members voted to join the Republicans and allow states in 2004 to hold their primaries and caucuses starting on the first Tuesday in February. Iowa and New Hampshire would continue to vote first, but other states would be allowed to move up a month.[34]

The most likely result of this change for 2004 is more primaries even earlier in the election year, presidential nominations that continue to be decided quickly, and yet again, few voters with a meaningful voice in the nominating process.

4

The Lay of the Land

2004

In some respects, the modern presidential nominating process resembles an iceberg. The shiny tip is the portion where the voters are involved in the primaries and caucuses. It is a period that in its entirety is several months long, although in reality the meaningful part has become compressed into a span of several weeks near the beginning of the election year.

The vast remainder of this imaginary berg, largely submerged from sight, is "the invisible primary" stage of the nominating process. It is the long prelude to the primary season where vital decisions are made that shape everything that follows. In spite of its importance, it is a stage where few voters are actually involved and not that many more are really tuned in to what is going on.

Some calculate the beginning of the invisible primary as the day after the previous presidential election. But the heart of this long opening round—fully a year long—starts immediately after the midterm elections. It is when the field of candidates forms (and sometimes contracts), and those that survive jockey for position in a way that will largely determine their success or failure in the presidential primaries to come.

Once the "visible" primary season begins, not all voters are equal. Essentially, they can be clustered into three groups in diminishing order of influence, depending on whether their state votes early, somewhere in the middle, or late in the primary season.

First up are the voters in Iowa, New Hampshire and a few other states that vote immediately in their wake. These voters could be considered the "kingmakers." In recent years, they have not only set the tone for the primary season, but essentially picked the nominees.

Next up are a group of voters that could be called the "confirmers." Their turn comes when the primaries move from scattered early tests to vast multi-front balloting on a single day. In 2000, the first and most important of those big single days was the first Tuesday in March. There, the confirmers can choose any candidate they want, but tend to ratify the choice of the kingmakers. In so doing, they bring down the curtain on the competitive stage of the nominating process.

Last to vote are the "rubber stamps," who are left with no real choice. In recent years, this group has included voters in more than half the states. Their role is simply a mop up one and their influence on the nominating process is nil. By the time it is their turn to vote, the nominations have been settled

The nominating function was once reserved to the parties' national conventions and the delegates that assembled there in the summer of every presidential election year. But that was in an era that is now growing more and more distant. Conventions still culminate the nominating process, but they now are merely ceremonial affairs. Not once since 1952 has a convention taken more than one ballot to decide its presidential nomination. And no convention has opened with even a scintilla of doubt about its nominee since the Republican conclave in 1976, when President Gerald Ford outlasted Ronald Reagan.

Modern conventions have become little more than giant pep rallies for each party, loaded with oratory but devoid of much meaning. Nowadays, they are little more than vehicles for each party to put their best face forward and every effort is made by party officials to keep any hint of friction—from debate over the party's platform to discussion of the future shape of the presidential nominating process—off camera.

As such, the conventions have become "made for TV" extravaganzas that even television, with the exception of a few high-number cable channels, has declined to carry anymore on a gavel-to-gavel basis. As coronations, they are no longer newsworthy.

Such a devalued role for the conventions is a recognition of the reality of the modern presidential nominating process, where the crucial decisions are not made at the end of the process but closer to the beginning.

THE INVISIBLE PRIMARY

The term "invisible primary" comes from a book of the same name written in 1976 by journalist Arthur T. Hadley. At the time, the nominating process was well along in its evolution toward its present form. A new system of public financing—with its strict contribution, spending and disclosure requirements—had just been installed. And for the first time in 1976, candidates were facing presidential primaries in a majority of states. "The race for the nomination had been made more complex, more tiring, and more costly," Hadley wrote back then. And it has gotten more demanding ever since.[1]

To Hadley, there were six tests to judge candidates during the invisible primary.

First, the psychological test. Does the candidate have the "fire in the belly" needed to navigate such a long and consuming process?

Second, the staff test. Does the candidate have managerial ability, reflected in his success or lack thereof in putting together a loyal, competent staff?

Third, the strategy test. Does the candidate enter the race with a road map of how to win the nomination or is he largely winging it?

Fourth, the money test. Can the candidate raise the money needed to compete in an environment where a reliance on a few "fat cats" has been replaced by the need to tap tens of thousands of smaller givers?

Fifth, the media test. Can the candidate make himself interesting and newsworthy enough to attract media attention?

Sixth, the constituency test. Can the candidate develop a community of energetic supporters willing to contribute to and work for his candidacy?[2]

Often, candidates will begin laying the groundwork for a presidential campaign years before the invisible primary begins. They frequently take a special interest in politics in the early states in the nominating process, such as Iowa and New Hampshire, appearing at party fundraising dinners, campaigning for state and local candidates, and funneling contributions through political action committees (PACs) they have formed to help further their presidential ambitions.

When the invisible primary season opens, the candidates attempt to harvest the fruit of their labors, often building their state and local organizations around politicians and party activists that they have already cultivated.

But the invisible primary is not a period where voters are engaged en masse. It is a time for candidates to build an organization, test their message, raise money, and find a niche for themselves, whether it is a distinct position on the ideological spectrum or the championing of a particular constituency group. The invisible primary is akin to tryouts in New Haven, before the candidates move to the political equivalent of Broadway—the presidential primaries.

For each potential candidate, the campaign begins with the elemental decision of whether or not to run for president. Two similarly ambitious politicians can reach two totally different decisions. In November 1974, for instance, Walter Mondale pulled the plug on a prospective presidential bid, subsequently explaining that he did not wish to spend the next year of his life "sleeping in Holiday Inns."[3]

Yet at the same time, Jimmy Carter was enthusiastically jumping into the presidential race. And he was not only willing to stay in Holidays Inns, but often spent nights in the homes of supporters, sometimes rising early in the morning to cook them breakfast. Day after day, Carter patiently practiced the art of "retail" politics, wooing voters one at a time or in small groups.[4]

The Last Straws

At the end of the primary season in 1976, Carter had amassed more than 6 million votes. That November, he garnered more than 40 million more ballots. But during the invisible primary, he measured his success in small handfuls of voters. That was often the size of the universe of party activists that took part in straw votes, one of the few samples of public opinion during the invisible primary that then and now involves real live voters.

In reality, straw votes have no relation to the delegate-selection process, but they can be immensely important in shaping early perceptions of candidates and their campaigns. As such, the most ballyhooed of the lot are given extraordinary attention by the media, something that Carter quickly realized.

He became an overnight sensation in October 1975 by finishing first in a straw vote taken at an Iowa Democratic fund-raising event. His winning total was in the vicinity of 250 votes, the size of many small hamlets in the Hawkeye State. But in an audience comprised of Iowa Democratic activists, where the tallying was done by the state's major newspaper, the *Des Moines Register,* Carter's showing demonstrated a degree of organization and support in the first caucus state that few suspected that he had.[5]

Straw votes, though, can just as often sink a candidacy as elevate one. Four years later, in November 1979, Sen. Howard Baker of Tennessee brought a planeload of reporters with him to witness his anticipated victory in a straw vote at the Maine Republican convention. To Baker's chagrin, he lost to George Bush, giving Bush an unexpected boost while inflicting a costly setback on Baker from which he never recovered. The total size of this political jury: barely 1,300 Maine Republican activists.[6]

And then there was the straw vote conducted by the Iowa Republican Party in August 1999. It resembled an old Cecile B. deMille cinematic spectacular, with the proverbial cast of thousands. Nearly 24,000 Iowa voters attended, many of them coming on buses provided by the candidates, and holding tickets priced at $25 a head that were bought and distributed by the candidates.

As it unfolded, the event looked at times like a Midwestern Bacchanalia. Outside the hall in Ames, candidates set up tents offering free food and entertainment. Inside the hall, there were fireworks, a balloon drop, a light show . . . and polling places.

In the end, George W. Bush finished with the longest straw, and expenses that totaled close to $1 million. Steve Forbes placed second, with a tab estimated to be close to $2 million. And more than a half dozen other candidates spent heavily to finish further down the list. Viewed as a precursor of the Iowa caucuses to come, it was an event that just one candidate, John McCain, felt he could afford to skip.[7]

Bush validated his position as the Republican front-runner, and Forbes, his status as a prime contender. But for others, the price of a poor finish was high. Former Tennessee Gov. Lamar Alexander, who placed sixth in the straw vote, quit the race two days later. By the end of October, two other seemingly formidable Republican candidates had abandoned their bids, former Vice President Dan Quayle and former Labor Secretary Elizabeth Dole. In essence, the Iowa straw vote had done what the Iowa caucuses themselves had long done, winnow the field.[8]

Democrats have had their share of straw votes over the years, but of late have actively discouraged them. Language in their party rules for the 2004 nominating process specifically criticizes both straw votes and "beauty contest" primaries (essentially non-binding popularity contests that do not elect delegates). Democratic rules call on state parties to educate the public that such events are "meaningless," and urge both state parties and candidates to "take all steps possible not to participate" in them.[9]

That has not stopped the media, though from doing some straw polling of their own. In November 2002, the *Los Angeles Times* published a survey of 312 of the 388 members of the Democratic National Committee (DNC), which found the party's standard-bearer in 2000, Al Gore, the tepid first choice of DNC members to be the nominee again in 2004. Gore led Sen. John Kerry of Massachusetts in the survey, 19-to-18 percent, with nearly half the respondents indicating that they hoped Gore would not run. Whether or not the survey had much impact on Gore, he announced the next month that he would stay on the political sidelines in 2004.[10]

A Time for Bucks, Not Ballots

In assessing the strength of the candidates during the invisible primary, the focus is often on two quantifiable yardsticks—polls and money. Until primary ballots start being cast, though, the public opinion surveys are often simply a reflection of name identification. Candidates that are already nationally known frequently rank highest in the early polling.

At the beginning of 1976, for instance, the front-runner among Democratic voters in the Gallup Poll was Hubert Humphrey, even though he was not running that year for his party's nomination. The Democratic favorite at the beginning of 1988 was Gary Hart, who had run a surprisingly strong race for the nomination four years earlier but had already self-immolated in 1987 when caught in an adulterous affair. And the Democratic leader in January 1992 was Jerry Brown, the former California governor who was in the process of making a quixotic third bid for the White House. None of the three came close to winning the Democratic nomination in the year in question (see table 4.1).[11]

In recent years, campaign fund-raising totals at the end of the year preceding the presidential election have proved a more reliable harbin-

Table 4.1. Winning "The Invisible Primary"

Voters play bit parts before the primaries begin, a period which has become popularly known as "the invisible primary." In the jockeying among the candidates during this long stretch, the focus is often on two quantifiable measurements—a candidate's strength in public opinion surveys and success at raising money. Candidates that are able to out-raise party rivals during the invisible primary and run well against them in the polls usually occupy the inside track when the primary season begins.

Victory in the "money primary" has been an accurate predictor of the eventual nominees since 1980. However, in both fund raising and the polls, the candidates ahead at the start of the election year have gone on to win their party's nomination nine of the 12 times there have been competitive nominating contests since 1976. That is the year partial public financing of presidential nominating campaigns was initiated.

The leaders below are based on the first election-year surveys of Democratic and Republican voter preferences in the Gallup Poll, and campaign finance filings with the Federal Election Commission at the end of the previous year. An asterisk (*) indicates the candidate was an incumbent president. A pound sign (#) indicates that he did not accept public funding. Only competitive nominating contests are included.

	Leaders in Each Party at Start of Presidential Election Year		
	Gallup Poll	Campaign Receipts	Nominee
1976 Democrats	Hubert Humphrey	George Wallace	Jimmy Carter
1976 Republicans	Gerald Ford*	Ronald Reagan	Gerald Ford*
1980 Democrats	Jimmy Carter*	Jimmy Carter*	Jimmy Carter*
1980 Republicans	Ronald Reagan	John Connally #	Ronald Reagan
1984 Democrats	Walter Mondale	Walter Mondale	Walter Mondale
1988 Democrats	Gary Hart	Michael Dukakis	Michael Dukakis
1988 Republicans	George Bush	George Bush	George Bush
1992 Democrats	Jerry Brown	Bill Clinton	Bill Clinton
1992 Republicans	George Bush*	George Bush*	George Bush*
1996 Republicans	Bob Dole	Bob Dole	Bob Dole
2000 Democrats	Al Gore	Al Gore	Al Gore
2000 Republicans	George W. Bush	George W. Bush #	George W. Bush

Source: Gallup Poll leaders are based on material provided by the Gallup Organization. Fund-raising leaders for the 1976 through 1992 nominating campaigns are from a chapter by Emmett H. Buell, Jr., "The Invisible Primary," in a book edited by William G. Mayer, *In Pursuit of the White House: How We Choose Our Presidential Nominees*, 13–15. The fund-raising leaders for the 1996 and 2000 campaigns are from material provided by the Federal Election Commission.

ger of success in the primaries. With the compression of more and more primaries into a brief period near the beginning of the presidential election year, the candidates need larger and larger quantities of money on hand at the outset of the primary season. And since 1984, the candidates who have raised the most money in the year prior to the primaries have gone on to win their party's nomination.[12]

Shortly after launching their campaign, every candidate faces a critical decision as to whether or not to accept public financing in the form of matching federal funds. Either way, there is a $2,000 limit on individual contributions (increased from $1,000 by the Bipartisan Campaign Reform Act of 2002) and a $5,000 limit on PAC contributions, although only a portion of individual contributions are matchable. Candidates that accept the federal funds—and the vast majority of candidates have done so since 1976—also agree to accept spending limits, which in 2004 are expected to be approximately $45 million. Candidates that do not accept the federal funds do not have to abide by the spending limits.[13]

Those who have declined the public money have had a checkered history of success. Former Texas Gov. John Connally was the first to do so when pursuing the Republican presidential nomination in 1980. He declined the federal funding, spent an estimated $12 million, and won one delegate. Forbes also declined public funds in his bids for the GOP nomination in 1996 and 2000, spending in the vicinity of $40 million out of his own pocket each time. Forbes was knocked out of the race early both years, winning only two primaries in 1996—Arizona and Delaware—and none at all in 2000.[14]

The conspicuous exception to this litany of failure has been George W. Bush. He declined the public money in 2000, far outspent his rivals who took it, and ultimately won the Republican nomination.

Bush ostensibly rejected the public funds so he could match the deep-pocketed Forbes dollar for dollar. Bush raised nearly $40 million by mid-1999, nearly $70 million by the end of 1999, and roughly $100 million by the time of the Republican convention in 2000. His total was roughly twice the amount that either Forbes or McCain could muster.

Bush's campaign took fundraising in the nominating process to Midas-like heights. Much of the money was raised by roughly 200 fund raisers within the Bush campaign called the "Pioneers," who collected at least $100,000 apiece in individual contributions of $1,000 or less.

With the new $2,000 limit for individual contributions, Bush as president is widely expected to raise in the vicinity of $200 million for the 2004 Republican primaries, even though he is expected to face no more than token opposition for renomination. For his reelection run, the Bush campaign has created a new set of fund raisers called the "Rangers," who are expected to raise $200,000 apiece.[15]

In a real sense, it is money that drives the modern nominating process. For the candidates taking federal funds, only individual contributions collected from the beginning of the year *prior* to the election are matchable. And with contributions collectable only in small chunks, that forces candidates to launch their campaigns and start raising money fully a year before the primary voting begins.

By the end of January 2003, a half dozen Democrats had already signaled they were running for president, with several others indicating that a decision was forthcoming. For those who lag in fund raising, the frequent reason given for their early withdrawal is a lack of money needed to compete.

ENTER THE VOTERS

When the curtain finally goes up on the voting stage of the nominating process, it marks the beginning of the end, not the end of the beginning.

Looked at from a distance, the visible portion of the process is a gauntlet of primaries and caucuses that is far more complex in its construct than the fall general election. The latter is a one-day nationwide vote on the first Tuesday after the first Monday in November, in which all registered voters may participate.

On the other hand, voting in the nominating process sprawls across the first half of the election-year calendar from January to June. Most states hold primaries in which voters cast ballots as in a general election. But a few states hold caucuses, which often take the form of neighborhood meetings, where voters kick off a multi-tiered delegate-selection process that can span weeks or even months.

The rules on voter participation in the primaries and caucuses vary from state to state. Some states allow the growing number of independent voters to participate in the nominating process. Other states do not. But the vast majority of the nation's 150 million or so registered voters have the opportunity to participate in nominating the president, whether they take that opportunity or not.

Kingmakers, Confirmers, and Rubber Stamps

Yet in reality, only voters in the first few states are guaranteed a meaningful voice in selecting the Democratic and Republican nominees. These voters—the "kingmakers"—were responsible for just 13 percent of the ballots that were cast in the major party primaries in 2000 (4.10 million), even though their votes in the critical events of January and February basically decided both the Democratic and Republican contests in favor of Bush and Gore (see figure 4.1).

Almost 44 percent of primary ballots (13.93 million) were cast on the first Tuesday in March. The large mass of voters that day could have steered the direction of the 2000 campaign away from Bush and Gore, but instead they were "confirmers," ratifying the advantage that the kingmakers had given each (see table 4.2 and figure 4.2).

Another 44 percent of primary ballots in 2000 (a total of 13.89 million) were cast by voters who were little more than "rubber stamps." They did not get a chance to vote until after the two major challengers, Republican McCain and Democrat Bill Bradley, folded their campaigns on March 9. More than two dozen primaries remained to be held at that point, but there was little left to vote for at the presidential level.

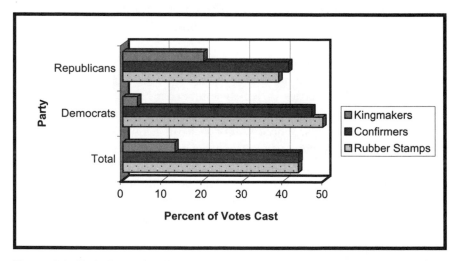

Figure 4.1 Early Primaries Most Important, But Most Votes Cast Later: The 2000 Presidential Primary Vote

Note: The bars reflect the proportion of Democratic and Republican primary votes cast in each stage of the 2000 nominating process. "Kingmakers" are voters in states that held primaries in January or February of 2000; "Confirmers" are voters in states that balloted on the first Tuesday of March 2000; and "Rubber Stamps" are voters that did not cast their primary ballot until after the first Tuesday in March 2000.
Source: Adapted from *America Votes 24*, 42–45.

Table 4.2.   The 2000 Presidential Primaries: Some Votes Worth More Than Others

The Democratic and Republican front-runners in 2000 positioned themselves for victory in the first stage of voting in January and February, knocked out their principal opposition in the second stage of voting on March 7, leaving votes cast in the third stage totally meaningless in terms of affecting the nominations.

In the vernacular of this book, the voters in the first stage are "kingmakers." Those voting in the second stage are "confirmers." And those casting ballots in the third stage are "rubber stamps." By far, the vast majority of primary ballots in 2000 were cast in the last two stages of the process, but voters in the first stage had the greatest influence.

The vast majority of primaries held in 2000 directly affected delegate selection. However, among the four Democratic primaries held during the first stage, only New Hampshire's actually determined delegates. The others were non-binding "beauty contest" primaries.

The Republican primary turnout in stage two included an estimated 720,000 votes cast March 7 in New York for GOP delegates, most of which were won by George W. Bush. However, New York Republicans did not have a direct vote for candidates, so these votes for delegates are not included in either the Bush-McCain percentages or the Bush plurality in votes.

			Republican Primaries			
	Number of Primaries	Turnout	Vote Percentage Bush	McCain	Winner	Plurality
Stage I: Kingmakers (through end of February)	7	3,596,047	47%	47%	Bush	2,689
Stage II: Confirmers (March 7)	11	7,355,092	57%	38%	Bush	1,272,903
Stage III: Rubber Stamps (after March 7)	25	6,924,978	77%	13%	Bush	4,450,350
Republican Total	43	17,876,117	63%	30%	Bush	5,725,942

			Democratic Primaries			
	Number of Primaries	Turnout	Vote Percentage Gore	Bradley	Winner	Plurality
Stage I: Kingmakers (through end of February)	4	507,631	56%	33%	Gore	117,377
Stage II: Confirmers (March 7)	11	6,572,487	73%	26%	Gore	3,111,523
Stage III: Rubber Stamps (after March 7)	25	6,965,627	80%	14%	Gore	4,599,443
Democratic Total	40	14,045,745	76%	20%	Gore	7,828,343

Source: Adapted from *America Votes 24,* 42–45.

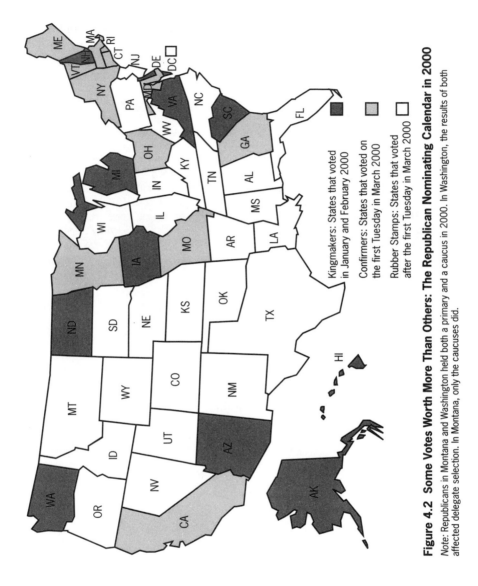

Figure 4.2 Some Votes Worth More Than Others: The Republican Nominating Calendar in 2000

Note: Republicans in Montana and Washington held both a primary and a caucus in 2000. In Washington, the results of both affected delegate selection. In Montana, only the caucuses did.

Kingmakers: States that voted in January and February 2000

Confirmers: States that voted on the first Tuesday in March 2000

Rubber Stamps: States that voted after the first Tuesday in March 2000

And there is no indication that this construct will be much different in 2004.

The tally above is based on the 31.9 primary votes cast in Democratic and Republican primaries in 2000. There were also nearly 2.5 million "informal" ballots cast in California and Washington for Democratic and Republican candidates outside the major-party primaries. Add those to the previous total, and the number of votes cast in the 2000 presidential primaries approaches 34.4 million.

Yet even with the more generous count, turnout for the 2000 primaries was barely one-third the number that turned out for the general election. The rate was slightly higher than that—35 percent—for primaries in the first stage of the process, jumped to 45 percent for the Super Tuesday primaries in early March, before falling to 27 percent of the fall turnout for primaries in the final mop up stage.

At first glance, these percentages may seem a bit counterintuitive. One would expect the highest turnouts among the kingmakers, since they had the biggest voice. And in truth, New Hampshire was the closest that any state came in 2000 to posting a general election-sized turnout. The number of voters who participated in the first-in-the-nation primary was more than two-thirds of the number (69 percent) that took part in the Granite State's presidential balloting that fall.

Yet turnout was much lower in the other February primaries because Democratic rules in 2000 prohibited states other than Iowa and New Hampshire from holding delegate-selection events before March, thus limiting competition to the Republican side of the ballot. In both Michigan and Virginia, for instance, the intensity of the Bush-McCain clash produced record Republican turnouts. Yet because neither state had a Democratic primary of note in 2000, the turnout in each was only about one-quarter of the number of ballots cast in November.

Turnout peaked on Super Tuesday in large part because of the high turnout in the day's dominant state, California. Including all ballots cast for Democratic and Republican candidates under the state's unique voting rules that year, the turnout rate in California was almost as large as New Hampshire (68 percent of the number that voted in the fall).

California employed a wide-open "blanket" primary in 2000 that encouraged mass participation. Only the votes of registered Democrats and Republicans counted for delegate-selection purposes, and they overwhelmingly favored Gore and Bush, respectively. But the rest of California's voters were allowed to cast non-binding ballots for the candidate of their choice, regardless of party. Roughly 2 million did, the plurality voting for McCain.

Also propelling California's turnout upward was the fact that, for the first time in years, the presidential primary had some meaning. In a bid to regain the luster it once enjoyed, state officials in 1996 moved the primary forward from its traditional date in early June to late March, then pushed it forward again to early March in 2000. As the anchor of the 2000 version of Super Tuesday, California voters possessed a voice in the nominating process for the first time since the Mondale-Hart contest in 1984.

For those citizens with little interest in the presidential race, the California ballot was crammed with contests for a variety of other offices and state ballot measures to draw voters to the polls. That stood in contrast to all the presidential primaries in February, which were freestanding events without contests for other offices on the ballot.

Yet in the end, when it came to defining their role in the presidential nominating process, California voters were confirmers, not kingmakers. By giving Bush and Gore landslide victories in their party's delegate-selection primaries, they helped bring down the curtain on the 2000 nominating contest with three months of presidential primaries left to go.

In the primary voting that followed, turnout did indeed drop. It dipped particularly low in states where the presidential primary stood alone, without the lure of state and local races to help attract voters to the polls. In mid-March primaries in Colorado, Louisiana and Utah, turnout was around 15 percent of what it would be in November. In other "stand alone" primaries held about the same time in Florida, Oklahoma, and Tennessee, the number of ballots cast was barely 20 percent of the general election total.

But as the spring unfolded, primary turnouts improved a bit, as voting was held in states that combined balloting for president with more meaningful primary contests for state and local office. The third-highest turnout of the entire primary season, for instance, was registered in West Virginia in early May, where the ballot included lively contests for governor and Congress. There, the primary turnout represented 56 percent of the number of votes cast in the fall.

Turnout measured 46 percent in Oregon in mid-May, where the

recent practice of conducting elections through the mail has boosted voting in the state's primaries and general elections. And turnout in Montana in early June was a respectable 49 percent of the fall vote, as the ballot in both parties featured spirited primaries for governor.

Still, the millions and millions of primary ballots for president that were cast after Super Tuesday merely rubber stamped the decisions that had been made in February and confirmed by primary voters in early March (see table 4.3).

The Inner Court of the Kingmakers

Iowa and New Hampshire are often lumped together when discussing the presidential nominating process. New Hampshire's preeminence as the nation's first primary state goes back to 1952, when the names of presidential candidates were placed on its primary ballot. Since the 1970s, Iowa has preceded it on the calendar as the first caucus state, making the duo a powerful one-two tandem in defining the presidential race.

Over the years, other states have sought to share the spotlight with the two early birds. In 1996, Republicans in Alaska and Louisiana held their caucuses before Iowa. In 2000, Alaska Republicans held their caucuses on the same night in late January that the Iowa caucuses took place. But GOP leaders in Cajun country and on the frozen tundra got little for their efforts, as the candidates and the media continued to regard Iowa and New Hampshire as the first significant vote tests of the nominating season.

Yet despite being paired together in the popular mind like bread and butter, the two states provide different venues with different systems of voting.

Iowa is a caucus state. Its event is a low-turnout universe dominated by party activists who are willing to take several hours of their time on a wintry night in January to attend one of 2,500 or so precinct caucuses around the state that launch the process of delegate selection. The Iowa caucuses are widely seen as a test of a candidate's organizational ability, as turnout rarely gets much above 10 percent of those who cast ballots in the fall.

On the other hand, New Hampshire is a primary state. Its event draws a much larger universe of voters, since the commitment of time required to cast a ballot can usually be measured in minutes rather than

Table 4.3. Highest State Turnouts in the 2000 Nominating Process

Not surprisingly, New Hampshire had the top turnout of any state in the 2000 presidential nominating process. The primary turnout represented more than two-thirds of all voters who cast ballots in the November presidential election in the Granite State.

In contrast, turnout for the Iowa caucuses drew barely 10 percent of the number that participated in the fall election in the Hawkeye State. Caucuses, even famous ones like Iowa's, traditionally attract only a fraction of the number of voters that turn out for a primary. The difference is often a matter of convenience. The commitment of time necessary to attend a neighborhood caucus can be hours, compared to the few minutes that are usually required to cast a primary ballot. The result is that every primary state in 2000 had a higher turnout rate than the Iowa caucuses.

Listed below are the 12 states that had the highest turnout rates in the 2000 nominating process, as measured as a percentage of the state's fall presidential turnout. All were primary states, although in only five did the turnout for the primary represent even half the number that participated in the general election.

There was considerable variation among the top turnout states in terms of when they voted, whether they were open or closed to independents, and whether there were other races on their ballot to attract voters to the polls.

In two of the states, Maryland and West Virginia, the Democrats held closed primaries in 2000 in which only registered Democrats could participate, while the Republican primaries were open to independents ("semi-open"). In Oregon, the situation was reversed. In the unique "blanket" primaries in California and Washington, voters had the option of casting a ballot with the names of all presidential candidates listed on it.

	Time Period	Voting Rules	Other Races on Ballot	Primary Turnout as % of General Election
1. New Hampshire	Kingmaker	Semi-open	No	69.0
2. California	Confirmer	Blanket	Yes	67.7
3. West Virginia	Rubber Stamp	Closed (D) Semi-open (R)	Yes	56.0
4. Washington	Kingmaker	Blanket	No	52.6
5. Ohio	Confirmer	Open	Yes	50.5
6. Montana	Rubber Stamp	Open	Yes	49.0
7. Oregon	Rubber Stamp	Semi-open (D) Closed (R)	Yes	45.9
8. Vermont	Confirmer	Open	No	44.4
9. Maryland	Confirmer	Closed (D) Semi-open (R)	Yes	43.7
10. Nebraska	Rubber Stamp	Closed	Yes	41.8
11. South Carolina	Kingmaker	Open	No	41.4
12. Massachusetts	Confirmer	Semi-open	No	39.7
Iowa Caucuses	Kingmaker	Semi-open	No	11.3

Source: Primary turnout rates adapted from *America Votes 24*, 9, 42–45. Caucus turnout rate for Iowa compiled by the author.

hours. The New Hampshire primary is widely viewed as the first true test of a candidate's popular appeal, and turnout is much closer to that of a general election.

While both are among the nation's smaller states—Iowa has just five of the nation's 435 congressional districts, New Hampshire has only two—they offer dramatically different backdrops.

Iowa is an agricultural state, but interest groups can have considerable influence by providing the organizational backing required for caucus success. Democratic candidates in Iowa often look to the left—to peace and environmental groups, as well as organized labor, especially politically active unions in the state such as the United Auto Workers (UAW) and the American Federation of State, County and Municipal Employees (AFSCME).[16]

Republican candidates in Iowa increasingly have had to tack to the right. In recent years, the GOP caucuses have been significantly influenced by the Christian right, which helped televangelist Pat Robertson to a surprise second place finish in the 1988 GOP voting, one spot above the party's eventual nominee, George Bush.

Iowa also is rooted in isolationism. According to David Yepsen, veteran political reporter for the *Des Moines Register*, the state was largely settled by Europeans who came to the agrarian Midwest to avoid wars and military conscription on the Continent. "We grow things here," says Yepsen. "It's a pastoral place. The idea of destroying things here is foreign."[17]

That makes the caucuses fertile ground for peace activists on the Democratic side, while the state's historic embrace of isolationism was evident within the GOP as recently as 1996, when conservative commentator Pat Buchanan finished a close second to Bob Dole in the party caucuses.

On the other hand, New Hampshire projects a more pugnacious image. "Live Free or Die" is the state motto. And with the large turnout for its presidential primary, the power of interest groups tends to be less than in Iowa. Entrepreneurial high-tech firms have come to define New Hampshire's economy as the old textile mills once did, and the religious right has never gained much of a toehold in northern New England.

While Iowa's leading newspaper, the *Des Moines Register*, has fashioned a moderate-to-liberal reputation, New Hampshire's major paper, the *Manchester Union Leader*, is stridently conservative. And for years, it was a power center of its own in New Hampshire primary politics, hectoring candidates to take "the pledge" to oppose imposition of a state sales or income tax. The *Union Leader* unabashedly promoted candidates that it liked and acerbically denounced those that it opposed.

In a scathing vernacular that reflected the paper's longtime publisher, William Loeb, Dwight Eisenhower was "Dopey Dwight." New York Gov. Nelson Rockefeller was "Rocky the Wife-swapper." Edward Kennedy was "the college cheat" and "the coward of Chappaquiddick." On the other hand, the *Union Leader* described Buchanan, whom the paper endorsed in the 1992 Republican primary over President George Bush, as "The Most Honorable of Men."[18]

The *Union Leader*, though, no longer resonates across New Hampshire as it once did. Loeb is long gone and in recent years Manchester has gotten its own television station, WMUR, which blankets much of the state. Many of the newcomers who have swelled New Hampshire's voter rolls over the last decade or two live along the state's southern tier and look south to Boston and beyond for their news. "They read the *Wall Street Journal*," says former Gov. Hugh Gregg, "not the *Nashua Telegraph*." Or for that matter, the *Union Leader*.[19]

The Power of a Few Votes

Parked at the beginning of the nominating process, Iowa and New Hampshire receive a disproportionate share of attention from the candidates and the media. That disparity between influence and population has drawn both states their share of criticism.

Yet each has jealously guarded its advantageous spot on the nominating calendar, helped by their supporters within the media. Reporters seem to have a particular soft spot for New Hampshire. "It's every reporter's dream," says political journalist Mark Shields. "It's small. It's close to Boston, and I can cover five candidates in one day." And in recent years, Washington journalists have been able to catch flights directly to Manchester, making New Hampshire very accessible.[20]

Like clockwork every four years, New Hampshire provides the media with an interesting story to cover. The state's independent, anti-authoritarian streak makes it an ideal spawning ground for the David and Goliath stories that the press loves.

Upsets have been the norm in the New Hampshire primary. Presidents have been humbled there. Front-runners have been derailed. Dark horses have been elevated. Every primary season, New Hampshire seems to provide a new surprise. As in Iowa, victory is less a product of large media blitzes than extensive one-on-one campaigning. And only a few thousand votes can spell the difference between a candidate being launched on the road to the White House or propelled down the slippery slope to political oblivion.

"Jimmy Carter won 35,000 votes in Iowa and New Hampshire" in 1976, says Shields, "fewer than it takes to be elected city councilman in Cincinnati."[21]

A few more votes than that are required to win both states nowadays. Al Gore took the Democratic contests in Iowa and New Hampshire in 2000 with roughly 115,000 votes, about 40,000 in Iowa and 75,000 in New Hampshire. But that was in a one-on-one contest with Bradley. The crowded field of Democrats shaping up for 2004 more closely resembles the size of the field that Carter faced in 1976, when he was able to prevail in both Iowa and New Hampshire with less than 30 percent of the vote.

Yet no matter how many candidates are running, the basic point remains the same as a generation ago. The swing of a comparative handful of votes in either Iowa or New Hampshire can made a huge difference in how the rest of the nominating process unfolds.

In 1976, for instance, Jimmy Carter won the Democratic primary in New Hampshire by just 4,663 votes over Morris Udall. Carter went on to win the Democratic nomination. Udall went on to a succession of runner-up finishes that earned him the nickname, "second place Mo."

The same year, Gerald Ford won the Republican primary in New Hampshire by only 1,587 votes over Ronald Reagan. Ford went on to the win the GOP nomination, while Reagan was forced to play catch up the bulk of the primary season.

In 2000, Al Gore defeated Bradley in the New Hampshire Democratic primary by just 6,395 votes, as close as Bradley would come to derailing the Gore express (see table 4.4).

Launching Pad or Last Hurrah?

But as often as not, the results in Iowa and New Hampshire are open to interpretation, which the media is more than happy to supply. Perception frequently trumps reality. In this environment, a winner can lose and a loser can win, depending upon the media's expectation and explanation of the outcome.

Table 4.4. Iowa, New Hampshire, and the Road to Nomination

With their position at the beginning of the nominating calendar, Iowa and New Hampshire are arguably the two most influential states in deciding presidential nominations. Yet the two states have chosen different winners in all but three of the 13 competitive nominating contests since 1972. Sometimes the Iowa winner has emerged the nominee; more often, though, it has been the New Hampshire winner.

Yet to win their party's nomination, candidates have had to finish near the top in both states. Since 1972, no nominee has finished lower than second in the New Hampshire primary, and only one nominee has placed lower than third in Iowa. The exception was Democrat Bill Clinton, who ran a distant fourth in 1992 after skipping the state in deference to its favorite son, Sen. Tom Harkin, who enjoyed an overwhelming home turf advantage.

In the early years of the Iowa caucuses, the "Uncommitted" option was preferred by Democratic voters and finished ahead of any of the Democratic candidates in 1972 and 1976.

Following is a list of the winners in Iowa and New Hampshire since the primary-oriented era of presidential nominations began in 1972. An asterisk (*) indicates an incumbent president. A dash (—) indicates that Iowa Republicans did not hold a vote in 1992. Only competitive nominating contests are included.

	Nominee	Order of Finish	
		Iowa	New Hampshire
1972 Democrats	George McGovern	3	2
1976 Democrats	Jimmy Carter	2	1
1976 Republicans	Gerald Ford*	1	1
1980 Democrats	Jimmy Carter*	1	1
1980 Republicans	Ronald Reagan	2	1
1984 Democrats	Walter Mondale	1	2
1988 Democrats	Michael Dukakis	3	1
1988 Republicans	George Bush	3	1
1992 Democrats	Bill Clinton	4	2
1992 Republicans	George Bush*	—	1
1996 Republicans	Bob Dole	1	2
2000 Democrats	Al Gore	1	1
2000 Republicans	George W. Bush	1	2

Source: Adapted from *Race for the Presidency,* 24, 29.

Solid second-place finishes against top-heavy favorites can make the runner-up look like the winner. That was the case in New Hampshire for Democrats Eugene McCarthy in 1968, George McGovern in 1972, and Bill Clinton in 1992, as well as Democrat Gary Hart in the Iowa caucuses in 1984. McCarthy, McGovern, and Clinton all lost by margins of nearly 10 percentage points in New Hampshire, while Hart finished more than 30 points off the lead in Iowa. Yet all four candidates received a "bounce" from their second place finishes that gave them momentum for the contests that followed.

The order in which the candidates finish is also closely watched and often determines who survives and who does not. "There are three tickets from Iowa to New Hampshire the day after the caucuses," explains Yepsen, "first-class, coach and standby." (22)

Since the primary-dominated era of nominating politics began in 1972, only one nominee has finished lower than third in Iowa. The exception, Bill Clinton, finished a distant fourth after skipping the caucuses in deference to its favorite son, Sen. Tom Harkin.

Meanwhile, no candidate since 1972 has finished lower than second in New Hampshire and gone on to win their party's nomination. But in recent years, victory by an underdog in the Granite State has not assured that candidate anything beyond a window of opportunity. And since 1992, as the primaries have piled up closer and closer to New Hampshire, that window has closed quickly.

In 1992, Paul Tsongas defeated Clinton in New Hampshire. But Tsongas found the value of his triumph devalued a bit by his perceived geographic advantage. He hailed from Lowell, Mass., just a few miles from New Hampshire. Tsongas would win only three more primaries, all in the Northeast, before suspending his campaign in March.

In 1996, Buchanan scored a narrow victory in a crowded Republican primary in New Hampshire, which turned out to be Buchanan's lone primary win of the year. Once the race boiled down to Dole and Buchanan, the well-networked Dole won easily and repeatedly.

In 2000, McCain trampled Bush in the Republican primary in New Hampshire by an unexpectedly large margin in excess of 40,000 votes. It was a wider margin than Ronald Reagan's one-sided victory over Bush's father 20 years earlier.

Yet even with the momentum of a landslide victory and the favorable media coverage that goes to a successful upstart, McCain would still have needed a long string of primary victories to stand a chance of winning the Republican nomination. That chance was lost two and one-half weeks later in South Carolina, where Bush got his campaign back on track with a hard-hitting victory.

McCain was able to match Bush win for win the rest of February. But for a challenger, trading victories with a front-runner is not good enough. In the modern nominating process, a challenger that wins New Hampshire must follow with a succession of primary victories that produces a quick knockout. Otherwise, as the primaries begin to unfold in rapid-fire order, the momentum that a long shot has generated can be overwhelmed by the front-runner's superior resources. That is essentially what happened in 2000.

"The McCain Primary"

McCain's candidacy, though, underscored a basic fact of voter participation in the primaries and caucuses. It is not just registered Democrats and Republicans who decide their party's nominations, but independent voters as well. By early 2003, the Democratic contenders were not only jockeying for money, favorable poll standing, and fresh ideas, but also the votes of the hundreds of thousands of independent voters who were the cornerstone of McCain's success in 2000. It is, wrote Shields, of this aspect of the early Democratic action, the "John McCain primary."[23]

If the Republican primaries had been limited to only Republican voters, McCain would have been forced to the sidelines much earlier than he was. Even in the stage of the primary season where McCain ran best—the first five primaries—Bush trounced him among Republican voters by a ratio of better than 3-to-2. But 30 percent of the votes cast in these early GOP primaries were by self-described independents, who favored McCain by a ratio of better than 2-to-1. And 10 percent of the Republican primary ballots were cast by self-described Democrats, who flocked to McCain by a ratio of 7-to-1.[24]

To be sure, independent voters cannot participate in all the primaries and caucuses. In close to 20 states in 2000, participation was limited to registered voters within each party. The list of "closed primaries" included Arizona and Delaware among the "kingmakers," Connecticut and New York among the "confirmers," and Florida and Pennsylvania among the "rubber stamps."

But in the majority of states, independents could participate in either party's primary, and should be able to again in 2004. Few states change their rules on voter participation from one election to another.

In many of the early states where independents are allowed to participate, their numbers could be significant. In Iowa and New Hampshire, fully one-third of the voters are independents. In California, more than 2 million voters are not registered in any party. And in Michigan, Missouri, Ohio, South Carolina, and Virginia, there is no party registration at all, giving voters wide latitude in which party's primary they cast a ballot. All are states that voted on or before Super Tuesday in 2000, and are expected to be near the beginning of the calendar again in 2004.

One caveat: Democratic rules require voters in their primaries and caucuses to have their participation publicly recorded, an attempt both to limit the events to registered Democrats and Democratic sympathizers, as well as to build a list of voters that the party can tap in the future. Whether that will tamp down the participation of independents in the Democratic primaries in 2004 is an open question. But with President Bush expected to glide to renomination on the Republican side, the only competitive action on the primary ballot is almost certain to be on the Democratic side.[25]

EXIT THE VOTERS

From the time the curtain went up on the 2000 nominating process in Iowa to the time the curtain came down on Super Tuesday was a period of just six weeks. The primary season continued for another three months and the Democratic and Republican conventions were held in August, two months after that. But the decisive stage of the nominating process was limited to that six-week period from late January to early March.

The meaningful stage of the 2004 nominating process could be equally short. There are always a few states that change their primary or caucus dates from one election to another. But the "front-loaded" calendar of nominating events in 2004 will probably be similar to 2000, with an even earlier starting date.

The Democratic National Committee (DNC) has approved a Jan. 19 date for Iowa and Jan. 27 for New Hampshire. It would be the earliest date the New Hampshire primary has ever been held, while Jan. 19 would match the earliest date for the Iowa caucuses. They were also held on Jan. 19 in 1976.

A potentially significant change in the 2004 primary calendar comes in the wake of New Hampshire. Last time, only Delaware voted in the 18-day gap between the critical Republican primary votes in New Hampshire and South Carolina—a lengthy span of time that probably cost McCain much of the momentum he generated from his New Hampshire victory. In 2004, though, the gap will be only one week between New Hampshire and the first Tuesday in February (February 3), when Democrats will now allow other states to begin voting.

The primary calendar will probably not be nailed down until the fall of 2003, as many states consider their options (see table 4.5). Some states that have held a free-standing presidential primary such as New Hampshire's may abandon their primaries altogether. Michigan and Colorado have already done so. With state budget constraints widespread and only the Democrats likely to have competition for their nomination, some states are viewing the elimination of their presidential primary as a way to save money.

Yet many states remain undeterred. Arizona, Missouri, Oklahoma, and Democrats in South Carolina (where primaries are customarily run by the state parties) have already scheduled their primaries for February 3. Tennessee and Virginia will hold primaries February 10. Wisconsin has moved its traditional April primary to February 17.

In short, Democrats in 2004 will have a steady staccato of voting from Iowa on. By the end of February, one-third of the states will have voted. By the night of March 2, more than half the country will have expressed their preference. By the ides of March, Democrats in two-thirds of the states will have held their primary or launched their caucus process. And it would not be a surprise if another state or two moved its event forward.[26]

No matter how the 2004 primary calendar finally looks, however, several factors could delay the choice of a Democratic nominee past early March. The absence of a clear front-runner could result in voters taking a bit longer to sort out the Democratic field. And Democratic delegate-selection rules could slow down a bit the rush to judgment. Unlike the Republicans, who allow states to award delegates on a winner-take-all basis, Democrats require their state parties to allocate delegates among candidates to proportionally reflect the primary or caucus vote, with 15 percent needed to win a share.[27]

Yet in recent years, nominating contests have been less and less about delegates and more and more about momentum. And in 2000,

Table 4.5. Presidential Primary Calendars, 2000 and 2004

The natural evolution of the presidential nominating process is reflected in the 2004 primary calendar. It is similar to 2000, but even more "front-loaded" with early events. An asterisk (*) indicates the Iowa caucuses; other caucus states are not listed. A pound sign (#) indicates that the event is likely to be a nonbinding (or "beauty contest") primary for the Democrats in 2004. A "(D)" or "(R)" indicates the primary was held by that party alone in 2000.

2000 Primary Calendar		2004 Primary Calendar (Tentative)	
Kingmakers			
		Jan. 13	DC#
		Jan. 19	IA*
Jan. 24	IA*	Jan. 27	NH
Feb. 1	NH	Feb. 3	AZ, DE, MO, OK, SC
Feb. 5, 8	DE (D), DE (R)	Feb. 10	TN, VA
		Feb. 17	WI
Feb. 19	SC (R)		
Feb. 22	AZ (R), MI	Feb. 27	UT
Feb. 29	VA (R), WA		
Confirmers			
Mar. 7	CA, CT, GA, ME, MD, MA, MO, NY, OH, RI, VT	Mar. 2	CA, CT, GA, ME, MD, MA, NY, OH, RI, TX, VT, WA#
Rubber Stamps			
Mar. 10	CO, UT		
Mar. 11	AZ (D)		
Mar. 14	FL, LA, MS, OK, TN, TX	Mar. 9	FL, LA, MS
Mar. 21	IL	Mar. 16	IL
Apr. 4	PA, WI		
		Apr. 27	PA
May 2	DC, IN, NC	May 4	IN, NC
May 9	NE, WV	May 11	NE, WV
May 16	OR	May 18	AR, KY, OR
May 23	AR, ID, KY	May 25	ID#
		June 1	AL, NM#, SD
June 6	AL, MT, NJ, NM, SD (R)	June 8	MT, NJ

Source: 2000 primary dates from *Congressional Quarterly's Guide to U.S. Elections,* Volume I, 404–9; tentative 2004 primary dates from the National Association of Secretaries of State (as of July 23, 2003) and the Democratic National Committee (as of July 15, 2003).

both the Democratic and Republican contests ended at the same time—shortly after Super Tuesday.

The Domino Theory

In the 1970s and much of the 1980s, candidates were less capable of scoring quick knockouts. Most of the primaries were held in the late spring and it was not unusual for the nominating contests to have an ebb and flow to them, replete with momentum shifts and a variety of primary winners.

In 1972, for instance, four Democrats won at least two primaries apiece, with George McGovern, Hubert Humphrey and George Wallace all winning contests toward the end of the primary season in May and June. In 1976, Republicans Reagan and Ford battled back and forth across the country, with both candidates scoring primary triumphs as late as the second Tuesday in June. And in 1984, Democrats Mondale and Hart similarly traded victories until the end of the primary season.

Back then, when a delegate majority could not be so quickly attained, voters in the later-voting states were more apt to exercise their independent judgment about the candidates and less apt to be influenced by the results from earlier contests. But with the primary calendar now compressed near the beginning of the election year, independent judgment has been a casualty.

More and more, it seems, voters have taken their cues from the media, who have taken over the role once filled by the party bosses of validating some candidates and dismissing others. Candidates that stumble out of the gate are usually dead in the water, as they lack the time and often the resources needed to recover. As a result, nominating contests since 1988 have been defined by a domino effect that amplifies the importance of early victories, with whatever volatility there is limited to the first few weeks.

In 1988, Republican George Bush swept every primary after late February, and Democrat Michael Dukakis won all but one after mid-March (losing only the District of Columbia to Jesse Jackson).

In 1992, Democrat Bill Clinton took every contested primary but one after the second Tuesday in March (losing only Connecticut to Jerry Brown).

In 1996, Republican Bob Dole's primary record was unblemished after late February.

In 2000, Republican George W. Bush's last primary defeat was on

Super Tuesday in early March, while Democrat Gore did not lose any primary or caucus that he contested all year.

In the modern nominating process, candidates can quickly get tagged as winners or losers. And, notes Shields: "Losing is the only American sin."[28]

WHO VOTES?

Voters who participate in the presidential nominating process never represent more than a small slice of the entire electorate, even using the turnout for the fall presidential election as the definition of a complete universe.

Only one out of every three voters who cast a ballot in November 2000 participated in the presidential primaries and caucuses.

Only one out of every six general election voters cast a ballot in the first six weeks of primaries and caucuses in 2000 when the nomination was still being decided.

Just one out of 25 general election voters were "kingmakers," participating in the critical February events in 2000 that preceded Super Tuesday.

And roughly only one out of every 200 general election voters took part in the process-shaping balloting that began the year in Iowa and New Hampshire.

In short, the voters who have the greatest voice in the nominating process constitute a tiny slice of the 100 million or so Americans who turn out in November to choose between the candidates that Iowa, New Hampshire, and a few other states have advanced.

The voters who take part in the early primaries tend to be older, better educated, and more affluent than those who comprise the much larger universe of general election voters.

In the November 2000 presidential election, a slight majority of all voters were from families with an income of more than $50,000. Half were at least 45 years old. And slightly more than 40 percent were college graduates.

Yet exit polls from the early events in 2000 showed that a higher percentage (fully 60 percent of the voters) in key Republican events in Iowa, South Carolina, and Michigan were at least age 45, as were roughly 70 percent of the participants in the Iowa Democratic caucuses.

In the vicinity of 60 percent of Republican primary voters in New Hampshire, South Carolina and Michigan had family incomes of more than $50,000, as did nearly 60 percent of Democratic primary voters in New Hampshire.

And in New Hampshire, a majority of both Democratic and Republican primary voters had college degrees, as did nearly half the voters that participated in the Republican primary in South Carolina.[29]

Mars and Venus

There have been some significant differences between the Democratic and Republican primary electorates evident in recent years. In the early events of 2000, for instance, there was a clear gender gap, with women comprising a majority of the Democratic voters in Iowa and New Hampshire, and men casting a majority of the Republican vote in both states.

On the Democratic side, the female tilt has been no anomaly. A compilation of primary exit polls by the *New York Times* in 1984, 1988, and 1992, found that a majority of the party's nationwide primary vote in each of those years was cast by women—54 percent in 1984, and 53 percent in both 1988 and 1992.

And unlike the Republicans, who have a primary electorate that is almost entirely white, the Democratic primary vote over the years has been racially multi-hued. How multi-hued, though, has varied from election to election, depending on the composition of the Democratic field.

In 1984 and 1988, for instance, when Jesse Jackson was running in the Democratic primaries, the *Times* computed that blacks comprised 18 percent and 21 percent, respectively, of the overall Democratic primary vote. In 1992, when no black candidate was in the race, the black share dropped to 14 percent of the party's primary vote. At the same time, though, Hispanics were beginning to appear on the radar screen, casting 4 percent of all Democratic primary ballots in 1992.[30]

Unfortunately, the *Times* did not attempt a nationwide exit poll summary of either the Democratic or Republican primary vote in 2000. And the only year the *Times* did a summary of the overall Republican primary vote was in 1996, and it was a bit smaller in scope than the studies of the Democratic primary vote in 1984, 1988, and 1992.

A Representative Slice?

One of the most intriguing and difficult questions to answer is whether the primary electorates of each party are skewed to the ideological extremes—the Democrats to the left, the Republicans to the right. It is a view that many political pundits repeat almost by rote, arguing that presidential candidates must tack left or right, as the case may be, to win their party's nomination, then must scurry back to the center to successfully compete for votes in the general election.

There is widespread agreement that voters who participate in the nominating process are more politically attuned than those who do not. "The people who regularly vote in presidential primaries are more interested in politics in general," says Austin Ranney. "Also, they are people with better formed and more elaborate political philosophies."[31]

But whether the primary universe is ideologically skewed is open to question, especially on the Democratic side.

An important question is skewed compared to what? The composition of a party's primary vote can be compared to a number of possible universes—such as a party's registered voters, its supporters in the November presidential election, or the complete universe of Americans who cast ballots in the general election. The latter is the focus of comparison here.

Exit poll data from the 2000 general election showed that roughly 50 percent of all voters were self-described moderates, 30 percent were conservatives, and 20 percent were liberals.

Yet in the key early GOP contests, the conservative share of the vote ranged from a low of 45 percent in Michigan to a high of 73 percent in Iowa. And in the critical Democratic contests in Iowa and New Hampshire early in the year, roughly half the voters in each state were self-described liberals.[32]

On the other hand, the *Times*' studies of the Democratic primary vote in 1984, 1988, and 1992, showed voters on the left to be a considerably smaller component of the party's overall primary vote than the exit polling in Iowa and New Hampshire revealed in 2000.

In 1984 and 1988, the *Times* computed that self-defined liberals cast barely one-quarter of all the Democratic primary ballots (27 percent each time), and in 1992 the liberal share barely surpassed one-third (35 percent). In all three years, the *Times* found a plurality of Democratic primary voters were self-professed moderates.[33]

Voters in Democratic presidential primaries "are not nearly as liberal as people think they are here in Washington," said Democratic consultant James Carville in early 2003.[34]

The prominence of Iowa may be one reason the nominating process is widely believed to be ideologically skewed. The state's low-turnout caucuses are easily influenced by interest groups on both sides of the ideological spectrum.

On the Democratic side, teachers, the public employees unions, the UAW, minorities, gays, peace groups, all are players. On the Republican side, there are evangelicals, pro-lifers and suburban business types. Yet the party "activists who go to the caucuses (in Iowa) reflect the activists in their party," says Yepsen. "They are the same constituencies that are active at the national level."[35]

Once the primary voting begins, it is arguable that pragmatism trumps ideology. For the candidates that have done best of late in the primaries have not been the ideologically pure of heart but those who are best funded, best networked, and most capable of rallying their party's base in its broadest form. Since George McGovern's ideologically driven candidacy in 1972, there has been a succession of reasonably close presidential elections between nominees of each party who were capable of appealing to the political center. In the last 30 years, only Reagan's victory over Mondale in the fall of 1984 was decided by a margin in excess of 10 percentage points.

CLUES FOR THE FALL

Even with its assorted flaws, the current system of primaries and caucuses always bears watching, for in the entrails of the vote are often clues to what will happen in November.

One basic rule of thumb is that the candidate who wraps up his nomination first is almost invariably the winner in the fall. Nominees that get bogged down trying to consolidate the support of their party's base have less time to woo the independent voters that are needed for victory in November. On the other hand, nominees that show broad appeal in their party's primaries are in a much better position to move on to the voter outreach that is necessary for a successful fall campaign.

Examples of both fates are strewn across the pages of recent political history. On the losing side were McGovern in 1972, Ford in 1976, Mondale in 1984. All lost in November after struggling to win their party's nomination. On the other hand, Carter in 1976, Reagan in 1980, Bush in 1988, and Clinton in 1992 telegraphed their November success with dominant showings in the primaries.

The whole idea of an early nomination leading to fall success is often referred to as "Donilon's Law," a tribute to longtime Democratic operative Tom Donilon who publicly advanced the concept. Stated succinctly, "Donilon's Law" says that "a party's chance of winning the presidency varies inversely with the length of time it takes its nominee to clinch the nomination."[36]

Applying this concept to the 2000 election, one could have readily predicted a razor close vote almost eight months in advance of the November balloting. For both Bush and Gore secured their nominations on the same day, March 9, when their major challengers abandoned the field.

There is little doubt that belief in "Donilon's Law" is a major reason that Democratic leaders decided to move up the start of their nominating process by one month in 2004 to match the Republicans. The earlier the process starts, the reasoning goes, the earlier it should be over, and the quicker the party can turn its attention to the fall campaign.

Incumbents, Renomination, and Reelection

When an incumbent president seeks reelection, the November outcome is often perceived as a referendum on his performance in office. And the ease or difficulty that the president has in winning renomination is often a reliable harbinger of his ability to win reelection.

Presidents who have faced little or no competition in the primaries—such as Nixon in 1972, Reagan in 1984, and Clinton in 1996—have gone on to win another term easily. They were free to focus on the general election at a time when the opposition party was just beginning to sort out its field of candidates.

On the other hand, presidents that face strong challenges for renomination are often defeated for reelection, as the scent of vulnerability wafting out of the primaries tends to only grow in the fall. It is the curse of William Howard Taft. And Ford, Carter, and George Bush have all experienced it in recent times.

It does not take long to gauge a president's electoral vulnerability. When it exists, it has been apparent in the New Hampshire primary. From Harry Truman on, every president who has won less than 55 percent of his party's vote in the first-in-the-nation primary has either been beaten in November or has dropped any thought of running for reelection altogether. On the other hand, every president who has won more than 55 percent in the New Hampshire primary has gone on to win reelection (see table 4.6).

Table 4.6. Gauging Presidential Vulnerability: The New Hampshire Yardstick

Since 1952, the road to reelection for all presidents has begun (and sometimes ended) in New Hampshire. Presidents that have easily won their party's primary in the Granite State have gone on to win reelection. Presidents that have received less than 55 percent of their party's primary vote there have either lost in November or decided not to seek reelection.

There have been five presidents on each side of the 55 percent threshold since 1952, although only one—Harry Truman in 1952—actually lost the New Hampshire primary. He was beaten in the Democratic balloting by Sen. Estes Kefauver of Tennessee.

The incumbent's vote percentage is based on all votes cast in the primary of the president's party in New Hampshire. The margin of the incumbent's victory or defeat in the nationwide popular vote in November is indicated in percentage points. For example, President Gerald Ford lost to Jimmy Carter in 1976, 50-to-48 percent, or a margin of 2 percentage points.

Winning less than 55% of the primary vote:

President	Party	Year	New Hampshire Primary Percentage	November Election Outcome
Harry Truman	Dem.	1952	44.2	Did not seek reelection
Lyndon Johnson	Dem.	1968	49.6	Did not seek reelection
Gerald Ford	Rep.	1976	49.4	Lost by 2%
Jimmy Carter	Dem.	1980	47.1	Lost by 10%
George Bush	Rep.	1992	53.0	Lost by 6%

Winning more than 55% of the primary vote:

President	Party	Year	New Hampshire Primary Percentage	November Election Outcome
Dwight Eisenhower	Rep.	1956	98.9	Reelected by 15%
Lyndon Johnson	Dem.	1964	95.3	Reelected by 23%
Richard Nixon	Rep.	1972	67.6	Reelected by 23%
Ronald Reagan	Rep.	1984	86.1	Reelected by 18%
Bill Clinton	Dem.	1996	83.9	Reelected by 8%

Source: Adapted from *Congressional Quarterly's Guide to U.S. Elections, Volume I*, 341–95, 677–87.

Glimpses of the Vast Mosaic

Yet New Hampshire and other early-voting states offer more than a big picture look at which candidates will survive. They also provide an early glimpse at the vote-getting appeal of potential nominees to the vast mosaic of groups that comprise the American electorate.

In New Hampshire, there are suburban voters who fill the towns along the state's southern border. There are blue-collar voters in the old mill towns that dot the state. And there are faculty and student voters in academic communities such as Durham (home of the University of New Hampshire) and Hanover (the site of Dartmouth College), who can provide both passion and shoe leather for presidential campaigns.

The Republican primary in South Carolina in 2000 demonstrated the power of the Christian Right. The 2004 Democratic primary on February 3 should give candidates their first test among black voters, who could comprise upwards of 40 percent of the party's primary electorate.

The same day, Arizona will expose the candidates in a growing Sun Belt state to a large Hispanic population. And Missouri should test their appeal in a state that not only defines the American heartland, but has been a bellwether in presidential voting the last century. Missouri has voted for the winning candidate in all but one of the last 25 presidential elections.[37]

Over the rest of February, the calendar of primaries and caucuses is expected to include Michigan, with its industrial heritage, heavily black urban center (Detroit), and large suburban vote in both affluent Oakland County and working-class Macomb County. Virginia and Wisconsin offer their own mix of populous suburbs, small cities, and rural terrain.

In short, if the nominating contests are indeed essentially over by the end of February in 2004, they could still provide some valuable clues about the candidates' vote-getting appeal. In the early primaries in 2000, for instance, George W. Bush demonstrated strength in the South and weakness in New England, strength in the rural heartland and weakness in the populous suburbs of the Frost Belt, strength among Republicans and tepid support among independents and Democrats. All were strains of voter behavior that were evident again in the fall.

But these early events on the nominating calendar still provide at most a sampling of voter opinion, since only a small segment of the country—or, if you will, the very tip of the iceberg—is usually engaged.

5

Looking to the World

How Other Countries Select Their Leaders

Among the countries of the world, the American presidential nominating process is "sui generis"—it's one of a kind. The United States stands alone in both the complexity and the scale of mass involvement in its presidential nominating process, even as its process clearly values some voters much more highly than others.

In other democracies around the globe, the system of nominating national leaders is much shorter, cheaper, and more tightly controlled by the political parties than it is in the United States. And voter involvement in the selection process, where it is encouraged, is usually limited to a party's rank-and-file members and not open to the electorate as a whole.[1]

Nonetheless, primary elections are increasingly being used to select candidates for top national office, although almost invariably a single nationwide vote is employed rather than the scattered array of state primaries that is used in the United States.

In countries with presidential leadership, elections tend to be held at regular intervals—six years in Mexico, five years in France, four years in the United States—and the nomination of presidential candidates precedes the general election vote.

In parliamentary systems of government—such as Canada, Germany, Great Britain, and Israel—elections can occur at four or five-year intervals, but as often as not are held on an "as need" basis at shorter, irregular intervals determined by the strength or weakness of the ruling party or coalition. Depending on the country, prospective parliamentary leaders are decided before the election or afterwards, the latter case if the party has suffered a particularly ignominious defeat.

In the United States, the parties have considerable freedom in developing their own rules, but there is more government regulation of the nominating process than practically anywhere else in the world.

Federal law governs campaign finance and state statutes set the ground rules for nearly all the primaries in the United States. As a consequence, political parties in other Western democracies tend to have freer rein to alter their nominating process with alacrity, and it is not unusual for two major parties within the same country to develop distinctly different systems of selecting their national leader.

Yet for all the differences, there are also some basic similarities in the nominating processes of the leading Western democracies.

Reform of the process, both here and abroad, usually takes place when a party is out of power and seeking means for an electoral comeback.

The role of voters in the nominating process, both here and abroad, has increased over the last generation, with a corresponding rise in grass-roots politiking, media advertising, and the other trappings of modern campaigning. It is not unusual to see American political consultants involved in campaigns in Great Britain, Israel or other leading democracies when not working for clients in the United States.

And throughout the Western World, the pool of prospective leaders is often limited to the most prominent figures within the political parties. Many must patiently wait a decade or more before attaining a position of national leadership.

Winston Churchill, for instance, spent more than three decades as a Conservative Party member of the House of Commons before being elected his party's leader (and prime minister of Great Britain) in the dark days at the outset of World War II.

Although Churchill's long wait may be an extreme example, the point is clear. In the world's leading democracies, political neophytes are rarely tapped. Since the end of World War II, the number of non-politicians who have been nominated and elected to their country's top elective office could be counted on one hand. Former General Dwight Eisenhower in the United States, lawyer Brian Mulroney in Canada, and Alec Douglas-Home in Great Britain (who was plucked from the House of Lords in 1963 to become prime minister, as well as leader of the ruling Conservative Party) are the most prominent who come to mind.[2]

This chapter takes a look at the nominating process—or leadership selection process, if you will—in a half dozen Western democracies: Great Britain; the continental European heavyweights, France and Germany; America's neighbors, Canada and Mexico; and Israel. While all of these countries have similarities in their selection processes, each is decidedly "home grown." And none of them have a process that comes close to matching that in the United States (see table 5.1).

GREAT BRITAIN: STABILITY AND CHANGE

Politically and culturally, the United States is an offspring of Great Britain. But from the start, the American system of government—and the presidential nominating process that goes with it—has been far different than in Britain.

Great Britain has a parliamentary system, with the top elected officeholder the prime minister. He or she is not elected by a direct nationwide vote, as is the president in the United States, but is the leader of the ruling party in the House of Commons, the popularly elected and most powerful branch of parliament

Also unlike the United States, the process of selecting party leaders in Britain is employed on an "as need" basis rather than at regular calendar intervals. And the contest often takes place *after* an election rather than before, particularly if the leader's party has just been defeated.

Occasionally, a leadership contest is triggered by a party revolt, as was the case in 1990 when veteran Prime Minister Margaret Thatcher was sacked by her Conservative Party colleagues. A contest may also be necessitated by the death of the sitting party leader—as was the case in 1994, when Tony Blair was elected leader of the Labor Party to replace John Smith, who had died suddenly.

Involving the Party Rank and File

Britain's two major parties select their leaders with input from their party's rank-and-file voters. But voter inclusion in the selection process has come only recently. The Labor Party added its party members to the mix for the first time in 1981. The Conservative Party, commonly known as the Tories, did not follow suit until 2001.

117

Table 5.1. Leadership Selection Process in Selected Democracies

Country	Governmental Structure	Party	Leadership Selection Process
Great Britain	Parliamentary	Labour	Electoral College
		Conservative	Party Membership Primary
		Liberal Democrat	Party Membership Primary
France	Hybrid (Presidential/ Parliamentary)	RPR—Gaullist Rally for the Republic (conservative)	Use first round presidential ballot as party primary
		Socialist	Party Membership Primary
		Communist	Party Membership Primary
Germany	Parliamentary	CDU—Christian Democratic Union (conservative)	Party Leadership
		SDP—Social Democratic Party	Party Leadership
Canada	Parliamentary	Liberal	Leadership Convention
		Progressive Conservative (conservative)	Party Membership Primary
		Canadian Alliance (conservative)	Party Membership Primary
Mexico	Presidential	PRI—Institutional Revolutionary Party (authoritarian centrist)	Nationwide primary for all registered voters
		PAN—National Action Party (conservative)	Party Membership Primary
		PRD—Democratic Revolutionary Party (social democratic)	Party Leadership
Israel	Parliamentary	Likud (conservative)	Party Membership Primary
		Labor (social democratic)	Party Membership Primary

Source: Adapted from James W. Davis, *Leadership Selection in Six Western Democracies.*

And in each party, members are only one part of the nominating equation. Since 1981, Labor has employed a tripartite system known as an "electoral college." Trade unions, rank-and-file party members, and Labor members of parliament (MPs) and more recently the European Parliament (MEPs)—share an equal voice in the choice of a leader.

In 2001, the Tories incorporated party members as the second half of a two-stage selection process, with Conservative MPs whittling the initial field of candidates down to two, and party voters deciding between the pair.

Yet there is no point in memorizing the rules of British party selection. The process for both parties is constantly evolving, arguably at an even faster pace of late than in the United States.

Until the mid-1960s, Conservatives picked their leader through a secretive process involving only the party's top leadership in parliament called the "magic circle." When the Tories were in power and their leader was also prime minister, their choice of a new leader had to be approved by the monarch. In 1965, the system was changed to give the nominating power to all Tory MPs, akin to the congressional caucus in the early years of the American republic, and Buckingham Palace was removed from the process.[3]

In the mid-1970s, Conservatives added a wrinkle that allowed sitting party leaders to be challenged, a procedure successfully used to oust Thatcher in 1990. After the Conservatives were driven from power in 1997, the system was changed again to the current one giving MPs the role of winnowing the field and party voters the power to make the final choice.[4]

In the meantime, changes in the Labor Party's selection process have been more incremental since they moved from a vote limited to Labor MPs to their current "electoral college" system. Still, there have been some noticeable changes in recent years.

Initially, the trade unions were given 40 percent of the "electoral college" vote, with the party's parliamentary wing and rank and file splitting the rest. In the early 1990s, the unions' advantage was eliminated, as each constituency was given one third of the vote. "One man, one vote" was also instituted within each constituency, so union leaders could not cast their vote as a bloc as big-city bosses used to vote their delegates at national conventions in the United States.

On a per vote basis, Labor MPs end up with far more clout than any other part of the party's coalition. When Blair won the Labor leadership in 1994, there were roughly 4 million eligible trade union voters, 250,000 individual party members, and only several hundred Labor MPs eligible to participate. It was calculated that the value of the vote of one Labor MP was roughly equivalent to the votes of 800 Labor Party members and 14,500 union members.[5]

Tony Blair and Labor's "Electoral College"

The need to woo colleagues in the House of Commons as well as voters in a much larger universe require candidates for the Labor Party leadership to display skill at both retail and wholesale campaigning. Blair excelled at both. Home secretary in Labor's shadow cabinet during the period of Tory rule, Blair ran a successful "inside-outside" campaign when his party's leadership position came open in 1994. He boasted the support of 135 Labor MPs, far more than his rivals, and mounted a high-profile campaign that underscored his broad popular appeal to a party that had not held power since 1979.[6]

The contest was the first in Britain to be so open, visible, and media oriented. It was likened by some British analysts to an American primary in its use of television, glossy print advertising and targeted mailings, as well as its emphasis on selecting a candidate that could attract swing voters to Labor in the next parliamentary election. The modern cast of the campaign suited to a "T" the telegenic and well-spoken Blair.

The contest, though, was much shorter and inexpensive than in the United States. Altogether, the period between Smith's death in May and Blair's election in July was barely 10 weeks. Spending by Blair was high by British standards, although it amounted to only $150,000 in American money, about what a presidential candidate in the United States might spend in the final days of campaigning in New Hampshire.

As for turnout, it varied dramatically by constituency. The total number of votes cast by the three Labor constituencies totaled just under 1 million, with roughly 70 percent of party members participating but only 20 percent of eligible union members. In an effort to save money, some unions did not send out ballots to its members. And to others, Blair's commanding lead served to reduce interest as did his calls to move the Labor Party toward the political center in opposition to the more left-wing agenda of the unions.[7]

In the end, Blair won the leadership contest easily, garnering a majority of the vote in all three Labor constituencies. He ran best among fellow Labor MPs (taking 60 percent of their vote), followed by individual members (58 percent) and union members (52 percent). That translated overall into a solid 57 percent of the "electoral college" vote, far more than the simple majority needed to win. The rest of the vote was divided between two rivals who were also mounting simultaneous campaigns for the position of deputy party leader (something akin to the American vice presidency).[8]

Blair proved to be an effective party leader. In 1997, he led Labor to a landslide victory that installed him as prime minister. In 2001, he led his party to another one-sided victory that maintained Labor's large majority in the House of Commons.

The Tory Two Step

The most recent Conservative Party leadership contest came in the wake of the 2001 parliamentary elections. Almost immediately after the ballots were counted in early June, Tory leader William Hague announced his resignation. That prompted the unveiling of the party's newly adopted two-stage selection process, which for the first time in Tory history included input from the party's rank-and-file voters.

In the first stage, Conservative MPs winnowed the initial field of five candidates down to two during a week of parliamentary balloting in July. In the second stage, the 320,000 dues-paying Tory voters chose between the two finalists, Iain Duncan Smith and Kenneth Clark. The latter was the better known of the two after years in the upper reaches of the party's parliamentary leadership, and with his personable nature was considered more popular with the British electorate as a whole. But Duncan Smith, a former army officer from the conservative wing of the Conservative Party, was considered a better match for the Tory voters who would decide the contest.[9]

Since this was the first time they were granted a role in the party's selection process, not much was known about the proclivities of the party activists who would make the final choice. However, it was widely assumed that they were on the older side (an average age of at least 60), were skeptical about Britain's integration into the European Union, and were generally to the right of Tory voters as a whole, not to mention, the entire electorate.[10]

The campaign between Clark and Duncan Smith was at times acrimonious. Besides their differences on Europe—Clark was far friendlier to the continent than his rival—the candidates were also surrogates of sorts for the previous two Conservative prime ministers, onetime allies now estranged. Thatcher backed Duncan Smith. Her successor, John Major, supported Clarke.[11]

But the campaign had its civil side as well. Both candidates agreed to a two-week truce in early August so they could take their families on summer vacation. And when campaigning resumed, both were able to stay within the spending limit of 100,000 pounds (roughly $150,000).

The vote was conducted by mail over a three-week period. And when the result was announced in mid-September, Duncan Smith had won 61 percent of the quarter million votes cast, with nearly 80 percent of party members returning their ballots.[12]

CONTINENTAL HEAVYWEIGHTS: FRANCE AND GERMANY

South across the English Channel, the French have developed a political process quite different from the British. While Great Britain has had a stable parliamentary system for several centuries, France's current system of government dates back to only 1958, when the Fifth Republic was formed.

It reflects the persona of its founder, the imperious leader of the French resistance during World War II, Charles de Gaulle, and was a reaction of sorts to the instability in the French system in the century before, when parliamentary governments rose and fell at frequent intervals.

The current French system combines a strong president—who is elected in a nationwide popular vote—with an elected 577-member parliament, called the National Assembly. It is led by a prime minister, appointed by the president, who is in charge of the day-to-day operation of the government. At first, presidents were elected to a seven-year term, but that was shortened to five years by a national referendum held in 2000.[13]

France: Personalities over Parties

Political parties were viewed by de Gaulle in a manner similar to America's Founding Fathers—with wariness and a sense of distrust. And his thinking has contributed to the development of a presidential nominating process in France that basically emphasizes "self nomination," with ambitious politicians often forming their own political parties or taking over existing ones as vehicles to promote their political careers.

Still, the French system does not encourage political outsiders to run for president. To get on the presidential ballot, a candidate does not collect petitions from voters but rather endorsements from at least 500 (of the 40,000 or so) elected officials around the country. And the candidates that have tended to do best in this system are those with active parties behind them and a long track record in French politics.[14]

In France's most recent presidential election in 2002, the three leading candidates were the incumbent, Jacques Chirac, the founder of the Rally for the Republic; Jean-Marie Le Pen, the founder of the right wing National Front; and Lionel Jospin, the leader of the dominant party on the French left, the Socialists. Jospin, at age 64, was the youngest of the three. And each of them had lost at least one previous bid for president, with Chirac losing twice before finally winning the office in 1995.[15]

Party-run primaries have been held on occasion to decide presidential nominations. On a February evening in advance of the 1995 presidential election, the Socialists held a nationwide presidential primary to choose a successor to their longtime leader and France's outgoing president, Francois Mitterand. The primary, open to the 103,000 paid-up Socialist Party members, was conducted at the party's regional offices around the country, and was won handily by Jospin, the former first secretary of the party.[16]

But as often as not, parties in France simply ratify the choice of their national leader for the presidential ballot without a full-scale vote of party members.

Under the French system, it takes a majority of the nationwide popular vote to win the presidency, which invariably takes two rounds of balloting. The first round serves as a primary of sorts to winnow the initial field of candidates—which can be a dozen or more—down to two finalists who meet in a runoff two weeks later. In most elections, that has meant the champion of France's center-right (de Gaulle's political descendants) versus the champion of the left (usually the Socialists).

The first-round voting in France's 2002 presidential election, however, did not produce the normal pairing. It was widely expected that the top two finishers would be Chirac and Jospin, reprising their 1995 presidential race that Chirac won by just 5 percentage points. But in the crowded first-round voting in April 2002, the controversial Le Pen's 17 percent share managed to boost him into second place behind Chirac, sending Jospin to the sidelines.[17]

In the short term, the success of Le Pen was a political windfall for Chirac. Widely pilloried as a xenophobic, far right extremist, Le Pen sent respectable French society scurrying to support Chirac. Rather than having to defend his long, checkered career in politics—which included two stints as prime minister and nearly two decades as mayor of Paris—Chirac was able to coast to a landslide runoff victory with more than 80 percent of the vote.[18]

But in other respects, the election was an embarrassment even to Chirac. In the wide open first round, where voters were free to back their first choice, Chirac drew only 19.9 percent of the vote, the lowest percentage polled by any sitting president in the history of the Fifth Republic.[19] And that was recorded against a backdrop of visible voter disinterest. Roughly 10 million of France's 41 million eligible voters did not take part in the first-round voting, a record high abstention rate for the opening round.

Much of the support Chirac gained in the runoff was of a grudging nature, with many voters talking of wearing rubber gloves or putting clothespins on their noses when casting their ballots for the incumbent.[20]

It is an open question whether these signs of voter alienation and disinterest will bring changes to the French electoral system before the next scheduled presidential election in 2007. But it is clear that the 2002 balloting did not work the way it was supposed to—with the primary-like first round giving voters the opportunity to blow off steam before they buckled down to cast a 'serious' vote in the runoff.

Instead, wrote *Washington Post* columnist E.J. Dionne in April 2002 after the first round voting: "This election shows what happens when there is more steam than seriousness."[21]

Germany: In the Heart of "Old Europe"

On the eve of the war against Iraq in early 2003, U.S. Defense Secretary Donald Rumsfeld dismissively referred to France and Germany as "Old Europe" for their unwillingness to join the American-led coalition.

While the overall accuracy of Rumsfeld's broadside is debatable, it does apply to the leadership selection process in Europe's most populous nation. The German process remains a relic of the past, a contrast to the gradual democratization that has occurred of late in many other Western democracies.

In the wake of their defeat in World War II, Germany adopted a parliamentary form of government that bears a similarity to the British system. The national leader in Germany is the chancellor, who heads the dominant party in the popularly elected lower house of parliament, the Bundestag. Voters do not directly vote for chancellor, casting their ballots instead for parties and their legislative candidates.

Ironically, leaders in the Bundestag are rarely chosen to run for chancellor. That honor often goes to a minister-president (or governor) of a German state or a big city mayor.[22]

Both major parties in Germany—the left-of-center Social Democratic Party (SPD) and center right Christian Democratic Union (CDU)—have a top down leadership selection process that closely resembles the long defunct "magic circle" of the British Tories. The tradition in postwar Germany has been for a closed door meeting of top party leaders to select a candidate for chancellor, a choice which is then publicly ratified at a meeting of the larger party congress.

The single break with this oligarchic tradition came in the early 1990s, when the Social Democrats—after a string of election defeats—experimented with a party primary to choose their candidate for chancellor. As an exercise in democracy, the primary was reasonably successful. Roughly 700,000 or so card-carrying party members cast ballots, a majority of the membership. But the practical result was the same as before, another electoral defeat for the Social Democrats. In 1998, the party returned to its old "papal style" selection process, minus the puff of white smoke.[23]

Yet in spite of the closed nature of the German system, party leaders often take into account public opinion polls and demonstrations of vote-getting ability in choosing their candidate for chancellor. In 1998, Social Democratic leaders united behind Gerhard Schroeder, the governor of Lower Saxony, immediately after he had guided his party to a decisive victory in elections in his home state.[24]

That fall, Schroeder led the Social Democrats to triumph at the federal level, ousting the veteran chancellor, Helmut Kohl. Schroeder's triumph was likened to that of Blair in Great Britain and Bill Clinton in the United States, as Schroeder successfully put a moderate cast on a party that had long suffered from an image of being too liberal.

Kohl had been the leader of a long-running coalition that featured his Christian Democrats and their Bavarian affliate, the Christian Social Union (CSU). In the wake of his defeat, the Christian Democrats were saddled with an image problem of their own as allegations of party slush funds overshadowed memories of Kohl's stolid 16-year chancellorship that included the historic reunification of East and West Germany. In 2002, party leaders took the unusual step of turning to the junior partner in the coalition for its candidate, selecting Edmund Stoiber, head of the CSU and governor of Bavaria.

In choosing Stoiber, an outspoken law-and-order conservative with the chiseled looks of an Alpine Barry Goldwater, leaders of the Christian Democrats turned their back on the head of their own party, Angela Merkel. As a native of the former East Germany and a woman, she offered something new in German politics.

But Stoiber was viewed as the stronger candidate of the two, having fashioned a flourishing "laptops and lederhosen" economy in Bavaria that contrasted with the bleaker economic picture across the rest of Schroeder-led Germany.[25]

Schroeder and Stoiber waged a nip and tuck campaign through the summer of 2002 that was ultimately resolved by Schroeder's greater ability to navigate Germany's "two and one-half" party system. Both the SPD and the CDU-CSU alliance finished with 38.5 percent of the vote in the September election.

But the SPD's coalition partner, the Green Party, drew a larger share of the vote than CDU-CSU's prime ally, the pro-business Free Democratic Party. That gave Schroeder a narrow majority of seats in the Bundestag and another four-year term as chancellor.[26]

AMERICA'S NEIGHBORS: CANADA AND MEXICO

The two countries that border the United States have had their nominating processes strongly influenced by the American experience. For much of the last century, the major parties in Canada have selected their party leaders through national conventions. In recent years, the major parties in Mexico have used nationwide primaries to nominate their candidates for president.

Both Canada and the United States were once colonies of Great Britain. But Canada followed a slower and more peaceful path to independence in which the British monarch is still recognized as Canada's titular head of state. As such, the Canadian convention system has been grafted onto a parliamentary government, with the leader of the dominant party in the popularly elected House of Commons serving as prime minister. As in Great Britain, parliamentary elections are held every five years, unless a government falls or the prime minister calls an election before the end of his term.

For the first half century after Canada attained self rule in 1867, leaders of the major political parties in Canada were also chosen in a decidedly British way, by caucuses of party members in the House of Commons, plus a few major party figures outside the parliament.[27]

Canada: Nominating by Convention

Yet the winds of progressivism that had brought presidential primaries to the United States shortly before World War I brought the convention system to Canada immediately afterwards. By the end of the 1920s, both major political parties in Canada at the time, the Liberals and the Conservatives (to become the Progressive Conservatives during World War II), had adopted the convention process for leadership selection.

Canadian conventions, though, have their own distinctive stamp. Candidates address the delegates before the balloting. Delegates vote by secret ballot, not by a roll call of the provinces. The candidate with the lowest vote total is eliminated after each ballot until one candidate wins a majority of delegates. And conventions are held only when a vacancy in the party leadership occurs, not every four years as in the United States.

As a result, Canadian nominating conventions have been few and far between. Since they were initiated in 1919, the long dominant Liberal Party has held just six nominating conventions at intervals ranging from six to 29 years. The party's last such convention was in 1990 when it nominated Jean Chretien, the current prime minister.[28]

Before the 1960s, Canadian conventions were comparatively small (no more than 1,600 delegates), quick to nominate (rarely taking more than two ballots), and apt to be compliant with the wishes of parliamentary leaders.

Since then, the conventions have grown to be quite large (3,500 delegates or more), more deliberative (often taking four or more ballots), and increasingly independent of the party leadership.[29]

The advent of television coverage in the 1960s was a major factor in the change. It transformed Canadian conventions from largely invisible affairs to highly watched cornerstones of the nation's political system. And the gavel-to-gavel coverage of the conventions tended to heighten the visibility of the party leadership position and increase the competition for it.

The dawn of the media age in Canada coincided with sentiment for increased democratization of the nominating process that was being felt across all of North America. In the United States, it resulted in a rapid growth in primaries. In Canada, it produced a dramatic increase in the size of conventions to accommodate greater rank and file participation.

With more delegates to woo, Canadian leadership campaigns over the last generation have taken on the characteristics of American presidential contests, replete with campaign consultants, pollsters, and self-starting candidates willing to traverse the far-flung country for months in the pursuit of convention delegates. Also mirroring the United States has been the increased cost in Canadian leadership campaigns, from next to nothing less than a half century ago to multi-million dollar price tags for recent efforts.

It is estimated that former Prime Minister Lester Pearson spent just $3,000 to win the Liberal leadership contest in 1958, the cost essentially of renting a hotel suite in the convention city. A decade later, the charismatic Pierre Trudeau spent about $300,000 to win the same position. In 1989, Chretien's campaign for the Liberal leadership cost an estimated $2.4 million. And in 1993, Defense Minister Kim Campbell spent roughly $3 million to win the Progressive Conservative leadership fight to succeed Mulroney. None of these figures may seem too lavish, until one considers that Canada has a population barely one-tenth as large as the United States.[30]

The 1993 election marked the end of an era in Canadian politics, as the ruling Progressive Conservatives saw their parliamentary total reduced from 155 seats to two, a drubbing of world-class proportions. The election left the Liberals in complete control of the federal government, the Canadian "right" badly fractured, and the Progressive Conservatives with the look of a spent force.

The recently formed Canadian Alliance Party, based in the prairies of western Canada, has displaced the Progressive Conservatives as the official opposition in the House of Commons. As a new party, the Canadian Alliance decided to use a nationwide primary, rather than the traditional convention, to select its leader for the 2000 parliamentary elections.

Balloting was conducted among the 200,000 voters who had paid a $10 membership fee to join the party. Polling places were set up in populous areas, while voting by phone was instituted to accommodate rural voters. About 120,000 voters took part in the primary and a subsequent runoff, which party officials estimate was about equally divided each time between those who cast their ballot at the polls and those who voted by phone.

The leadership contest was ultimately won by Stockwell Day, a flat tax advocate and social conservative from the western province of Alberta. He proved to be a controversial choice who was effectively dismissed by Chretien as to "the right of the right of the right." The Canadian Alliance gained a handful of seats in the 2000 elections, but failed to make significant inroads in populous Ontario, and Day subsequently resigned his leadership post.[31]

Yet the role of the primary in leadership selection seems to have taken root in Canada. The Canadian Alliance conducted a leadership primary entirely by mail ballot in 2002, which drew an even higher rate of participation than the party's initial vote two years earlier.[32]

And while Liberals will continue to use a convention to select their leader, they have adopted a plan to hold local primaries across the country to select delegates in each of the roughly 300 parliamentary districts (called ridings). Delegates will be divided proportionally among the candidates to reflect their share of the vote in each riding. The first test of the Liberals' new primary-convention system is scheduled to come in November 2003, when a national leadership convention will be held to choose a successor to the retiring Chretien.[33]

Chretien's long run as head of the Liberal Party and his decade as prime minister has not been marked by an era of good feelings in Canadian politics. The craggy Chretien has made his share of enemies, even within his own party. Before he announced that he would step down in early 2004, he faced the prospect of a party "leadership review" similar to the device that British Tories used to dump Prime Minister Thatcher in the midst of her term. By announcing his retirement, Chretien spared himself from facing a vote of confidence within his own party that he may not have survived.[34]

Mexico: From Tightly Closed to Wide Open

Probably no democratic country has undergone a quicker and more dramatic evolution in its nominating process than Mexico. In the course of just one election, its process changed from being tightly closed to wide open, with both the long-dominant Institutional Revolutionary Party (PRI) and the leading opposition party, the National Action Party (PAN), instituting nationwide primaries to nominate their candidates for Mexico's 2000 presidential election.

The PRI had controlled the presidency of Mexico since 1929, and during that long tenure the incumbent had selected his successor through a secretive process called "dedazo," or the "fingering" of an heir apparent. But by the late twentieth century, the PRI was losing ground across Mexico and their nominating process, as it was, was widely seen as too autocratic and too antiquated for a country with 50 million voters.

Outgoing President Ernesto Zedillo announced in 1999 that he would break with the customary practice and not handpick his party's standard-bearer in the 2000 election. Instead he proposed that the party hold a nationwide primary, which was approved overwhelmingly by PRI officials.[35]

Restrictions were placed on who could run. Religious ministers, members of the military, and former presidents were all ruled out. Otherwise, the contest for the PRI nomination produced an American-style campaign with media advertising, a nationally televised debate, and plenty of charges of negative campaigning.[36]

But the rules of the balloting were more like an American general election than a primary. The nominee was determined by who carried the most electoral districts, not who won the popular vote, although in the PRI's first-ever primary in November 1999, both were won by the same candidate, Zedillo's former interior minister, Francisco Labastida. He won a slim majority of the more than nine million votes cast but swept more than 90 percent of the 300 electoral districts.[37]

Meanwhile, the PAN, which had previously chosen its nominees through a convention, also switched to a nationwide primary to select its leader. Voter participation, though, was limited to its 350,000 party members, of which barely 130,000 took part. Non-members were allowed to cast "informal" ballots that were tallied separately.[38]

As an exercise in democracy, the PAN primary was not that noteworthy. With an early start that mirrored presidential campaigns north of the border, Vincente Fox cleared the field of potential rivals and won his party's primary unopposed.

Still, the willingness of Mexico's two major parties to select their presidential candidates by primary vote marked a huge transformation in the country's nominating process. Virtually overnight, rank-and-file voters went from being spectators to active participants. The following July, the history-making continued as Fox—a former Coca Cola executive and Mexican state governor—won the presidency, bringing down the curtain on the PRI's 71-year control of Mexico's top office.

ISRAEL: AN OASIS OF DEMOCRACY

All of the countries featured so far in this chapter border democracies. Not so the nation of Israel, which is an oasis of democracy in the Middle East. Barely a half century old, the Jewish state is an experiment both culturally and politically.

Like much of Western Europe, Israel has a parliamentary system of government headed by a prime minister. From 1996 to 2001, Israel experimented with the direct election of its prime minister by nationwide vote. But after the 2001 election, in which Ariel Sharon ousted Ehud Barak, Israel returned to a more traditional form of voting for parliament (called the Knesset), with the party with the most seats forming the government and its leader becoming prime minister.[39]

However, both of Israel's two major parties, the hawkish Likud Party and the more dovish Labor Party, hold primary elections among party members to select their candidates for prime minister. Both parties held leadership primaries in November 2002 in the midst of Israel's recent round of bloody conflict with the Palestinians, with the contests in both parties focusing on internal security and the appropriate response to attacks by Palestinian terrorists.

The Likud primary contest was a battle between two political titans, Prime Minister Sharon and former Prime Minister Benjamin Netanyahu, who Sharon had brought into his cabinet as foreign minister on the eve of the party vote. Netanyahu tried to position himself to the right of Sharon, arguing that Israel needed to toughen its response to Arab terrorists. If elected, Netanyahu promised his first act would be to expel Palestinian leader Yasir Arafat from his headquarters on the occupied West Bank.[40]

131

Enjoying high approval ratings for his forceful response to terrorist attacks, Sharon dismissed his longtime rival as reckless and rash. Likud voters tended to agree. Slightly less than half of the eligible primary electorate—300,000 fee-paying Likud members—cast ballots. But those that did favored Sharon over Netanyahu by a margin of nearly 3-to-2.[41]

Voting took place at 678 polling places across Israel. At one of them, a Likud Party headquarters in the northern Israeli community of Beit Shean, the violence that served as a backdrop for the campaign was felt directly. Two Palestinian gunmen opened fire on primary voters and local party workers, killing at least six before being killed themselves.[42]

The Labor Party primary was held barely one week earlier, but was far different from the Likud contest in both its tone and result. The leading Labor contenders were Haifa Mayor Amram Mitzna, a former general who ran as a peace candidate, and incumbent Labor Party leader, Binyamin Ben-Eliezer, who had served as defense minister in a Sharon-led coalition government that had collapsed earlier in the fall of 2002.

While the Likud leadership primary featured two strong-willed personalities, the Labor primary underscored elemental policy differences within the left-of-center party. Mitzna claimed that the Labor Party had been co-opted by participation in the Likud-led coalition and that peace with the Palestinians would come only through negotiation, not the use of force. Ben-Eliezer maintained that Labor's presence in the Sharon government was a moderating element and that it had helped position the party closer to Israel's security-conscious political mainstream.

But the Labor Party mainstream was clearly to the left of Ben-Eliezer. And among the 120,000 party members eligible to vote in the primary, Mitzna triumphed by a margin of nearly 3-to-2. He easily cleared the 40 percent threshold required of winning Labor Party leadership candidates to avoid a runoff.[43]

As it turned out, Mitzna's victory in the leadership primary was a personal high-water mark, as Sharon led Likud to a clear-cut victory over Labor in the January 2003 elections for seats in the Knesset.

Yet at least Mitzna's victory in the Labor Party primary was clear of the type of controversy that had clouded Ben-Eliezer's election as party leader the previous year. Roiled by charges of voting fraud, the leadership contest had required two primary votes.

In the first primary held in September 2001, Avraham Burg, the speaker of the Knesset, led Ben-Eliezer by roughly 1,000 votes out of more than 70,000 votes cast when party officials suspended the vote count amid charges by Ben-Eliezer of voting irregularities. Ben-Eliezer subsequently emerged the winner after party officials decided to hold another primary that December in several dozen polling places where the initial vote had been contested.[44]

Ben-Eliezer denounced the initial primary vote as a "theft." Burg dismissed the primary 're-vote' as "a farce." But possibly the unkindest cut of all—at least from an American perspective—came from Israeli political pundits who compared the Labor Party imbroglio to the complex, confusing and ultimately judicially settled U.S. presidential vote count the previous year. It was, they said, the latest example of a "Florida syndrome."[45]

6

Can We Do Better Than This?

Hardly anyone is a fan of the current presidential nominating process. The feedback one hears is sometimes colorful, nearly always critical, and ranges from a sense of exasperation to hopelessness that the process can ever be changed for the better.

When asked about the current process, long-time political observers often respond with comments that are pungent and starkly negative. "It's nuts . . . It's awful . . . It is a mindless dash . . . It defies rationality . . . It has changed for the worse . . . It is beyond fixing," are just some of the printable responses that this author has heard.

One of the basic problems is that most everywhere else around the world, political parties draw up their own nominating processes and are solely responsible for operating them.

But in the United States, control of the process is not so clear-cut. There are a number of players—the national and state parties, the state governments, and potentially, Congress (which has already defined the sphere of campaign finance). This cast of characters is rarely, if ever, on the same page when it comes to the proper course of action. As a result, inertia tends to prevail in the short run and incremental evolution wins out in the long run.

That is particularly the case headed into the middle of the first decade of the 21st century. Over the last generation, it has been the party out of power that has been the engine of reform. A party's failure in November is often blamed on its nominating process, and defeat can trigger a desire for change that victory usually mutes.

But both parties came out of the 2000 presidential election arguing that they had won, with Republicans taking the critical electoral vote but Democrats carrying the nationwide popular vote. As a result, the cry for a wholesale restructuring of the nominating process, which was heard in both parties before the 2000 election, was replaced afterward with a tweak here and a tinker there, producing the latest bit of incremental evolution.

Throughout the nation's history, the few big changes in the nominating process have come a decade or more after criticism with the existing system began to fester. Attacks on the congressional caucus as a viable nominating vehicle were heard as early as the first decade of the nineteenth century, but conventions did not publicly appear to replace them until the early 1830s. Criticism of conventions as "boss ridden" was audible by the late nineteenth century, but it was not until 1912 that presidential primaries appeared on a grand scale. And while criticism with the primary-convention system (with emphasis on the latter) exploded in 1968, it was not until 1976 that a majority of states were holding presidential primaries, putting an exclamation point on the primaries' newfound dominance of the nominating process.

A TRIO OF PROPOSALS

Nowadays, plans abound to revamp the nominating process. Some proposals—such as a national primary, a rotating system of regional primaries, and the calendar arrangement of states in reverse order of their population—have already garnered a fair degree of national attention. In addition, there are a number of less discussed plans that have served to make the overhaul of the presidential nominating process a budding cottage industry.

There is a proposal for time zone primaries, where states in the same time zone would vote on the same date. There is a plan for a pre-primary convention, a reversal of the current order where a party's national convention would winnow the field of candidates and voters would then make the final choice in a nationwide primary. And for those who like gambling, there is the lottery system proposal, where up to three states could a hold primary or caucus each week, and if more than three wanted the same week, the choice would be made by lottery.[1]

Still, there is widespread feeling among many political observers that the nation may be headed inexorably toward a national primary, at least a de facto one. In 2000, more than a dozen states held primaries or caucuses on the first Tuesday in March, including California, New York,

Ohio, Georgia, Maryland, and all of the New England states except New Hampshire. A similar pileup is shaping up for 2004, with an additional dozen or so states expected to vote in a six-week span before the big single day votefest in early March.[2]

A National Primary: The People's Choice

If a one-day nationwide primary vote is ultimately adopted, it would probably be okay with most American voters. They have given their overwhelming approval to the concept in an array of Gallup Polls taken from 1952 through 1988. Support for a national primary has ranged from a low of 56 percent in the mid-1950s to 76 percent in the wake of the tumultuous 1968 Democratic convention in Chicago. Opposition to the idea during this 36-year span never exceeded 27 percent.

Critics argue that support for a national primary may be broad but it is not deep. There were signs of ambivalence in a pair of Gallup Polls taken in the summer of 1964. While the national primary idea was favored then by a margin in excess of 2-to-1, nearly 60 percent of respondents said they did not want to see any changes made to the national conventions, where nominations then were decided.[3]

Still, the reasons for broad-based support for a one-day national primary are fairly obvious. It has the virtue of simplicity, and in an era where democracy (in terms of "one person, one vote") is depicted as the ideal, a national primary provides it in its most direct form. The concept of a national primary is much easier to understand than other alternatives (or the present system, for that matter). And it parallels the way nominations for practically every other office in the United States are decided.

Clearly, a national primary would eliminate concerns over frontloading and the advantage held by early-voting states such as Iowa and New Hampshire. It would make all votes meaningful since they would be cast concurrently and tallied on a national basis. And it would likely increase voter participation, since interest would be focused on a single event in which the whole country could participate, just like the November general election.

Supporters of a national primary also argue that such an event would possibly shorten presidential campaigns, since the long primary season would be truncated into one day, probably in July or August of the presidential election year. Even if no candidate won a majority of the vote and a runoff between the top two was required, a second vote most likely would take place within a few weeks of the initial vote (see table 6.1).

There are concerns that a one-day national primary would stack the deck in favor of the best-known and best-financed contenders. Unless Iowa and New Hampshire were given special exemptions to retain their leadoff spots, there would be no small states at the beginning of the process to offer a level playing field and allow a dark horse candidate to make an impression.

The cost of campaigning could be more expensive with a national primary, since lavish advertising campaigns in major media markets across the country would be required. And attention would have to be focused on the most populous areas of the country where voters are clustered in large numbers. The retail campaigning required to compete in small states such as Iowa and New Hampshire would be a thing of the past.

In the wake of the contentious ending to the 2000 presidential election, there is the additional question of whether a national primary could produce a legitimate nominee if the vote was extremely close. Under the Electoral College system used to *elect* the president, the conflict in 2000 was confined to Florida, and even there, the focus was on the vote in a few counties. A closely contested national primary, though, could require a nationwide recount involving tens of millions of votes. That would make the Florida imbroglio of 2000 look like child's play.

Then there is the basic question of the role of the parties if a national primary was instituted. Currently, the national parties set the ground rules for their presidential nominating process and organize the national convention that culminates it. The state parties and state election administrators fill in the blanks.

With a national primary, the role of the state election administrators would move front and center. But the role of the parties, state and national, would be more nebulous. The need for a convention would appear optional, although some political observers see the quadrennial gathering of the party faithful as having much the same role that it does now—as a giant pep rally to introduce the presidential ticket to the American electorate, and as a forum to draw up a platform and discuss party rules.[4]

Table 6.1. Hypothetical National Primaries, Hypothetical Runoffs

To be sure, the dynamic of a national primary would be quite different than the rolling series of primary elections that have been the centerpiece of the presidential nominating process since 1972. But by aggregating the vote from the primaries each year since then, one gets a rough approximation of what the vote in a national primary might look like (albeit a smaller version, since never have all the states held primary elections).

Using actual primary results as the basis of a hypothetical national primary, no Republican nominating contest since 1972 would have required a runoff, assuming a 50 percent standard is used. The GOP nominee each time drew a majority of the Republican primary vote, including President Gerald Ford, who won 53 percent in his two-way battle with Ronald Reagan in 1976.

On the other hand, four of the Democratic contests would have required runoffs: between Hubert Humphrey and George McGovern in 1972; Jimmy Carter and Jerry Brown in 1976; Walter Mondale and Gary Hart in 1984; and Michael Dukakis and Jesse Jackson in 1988.

The aggregate nationwide Democratic primary vote in each of these four nominating contests is listed below. A pound sign (#) indicates candidates that would have qualified for a hypothetical runoff. An asterisk (*) indicates the actual nominee. Other candidates that received at least 10 percent of the Democratic primary vote in each of these years are also listed.

1972 Democrats	Total Vote	Percentage
Hubert Humphrey #	4,121,372	26
George McGovern # *	4,053,451	25
George Wallace	3,755,424	24
Edmund Muskie	1,840,217	12
Others	2,223,501	14
Total Vote	15,993,965	
1976 Democrats		
Jimmy Carter # *	6,235,609	39
Jerry Brown #	2,449,374	15
George Wallace	1,995,388	12
Morris Udall	1,611,754	10
Others	3,760,527	23
Total Vote	16,052,652	
1984 Democrats		
Walter Mondale # *	6,811,214	38
Gary Hart #	6,503,968	36
Jesse Jackson	3,282,380	18
Others	1,411,630	8
Total Vote	18,009,192	
1988 Democrats		
Michael Dukakis # *	9,817,185	43
Jesse Jackson #	6,685,699	29
Al Gore	3,134,516	14
Others	3,324,536	14
Total Vote	22,961,936	

Source: Adapted from *Race for the Presidency*, 144, 146, 150, 152.

Regional Primaries: The Choice of Election Administrators

The national primary idea has polled well among the public at large, less so among political professionals and those who tend to pay the most attention to the nominating process. A 1982 Gallup Poll of "Opinion Leaders" found less than majority support for the concept.[5]

Among those not enthused by a national primary were the nation's leading election administrators. Their organization, the National Association of Secretaries of State (NASS), have formally put forward a plan of their own that builds on the idea of regional primaries. Under the NASS proposal, Iowa and New Hampshire would be allowed to keep their leadoff spots, while the rest of the country would be grouped into four regions—the East, South, Midwest and West.

The first year the plan would be in effect, the East would vote in March, the South in April, the Midwest in May, and the West in June. In the next election cycle, the East would drop back to the end of the calendar in June, the South would move up to March, and every other region would move forward a month as well. The regional rotation would continue every four years, so that over a period of four election cycles, every region would have a chance to vote first (see figure 6.1).[6]

Proponents of the rotating regional primary plan claim that it is a fair antidote to the current front-loaded primary system, where year after year the spotlight often falls on the same array of early-voting states. Regional primaries, they argue, should keep down the costs of campaigning since the states within each region would be in relatively close proximity, and some major media markets would overlap several states, giving candidates more bang for their advertising buck.

The proposal is also seen by its backers as a natural step in the evolution of the current presidential primary system, which has featured a conspicuous number of voluntarily formed regional primaries over the last quarter century. Only once, in 1988, has one region (the South) come close to voting together as a group, as NASS proposes with its plan. But smaller-sized regions have been a staple of the primary calendar in recent years. In 1996, a series of small to mid-size regional primaries—in New England, the South, the industrial Midwest and the Pacific West—filled the month of March. In 2004, seven states in the Northeast are scheduled to vote on the first Tuesday in March. Three states in the South are slated to vote a week later.

The rotating regional primary plan is not without controversy.

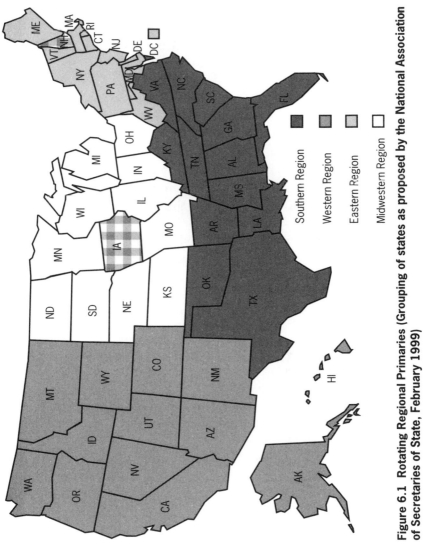

Figure 6.1 Rotating Regional Primaries (Grouping of states as proposed by the National Association of Secretaries of State, February 1999)

Note: Under this plan, Iowa and New Hampshire would be allowed to continue holding their leadoff spots in the nominating process.

Each region would offer roughly 25 percent of the delegates—enabling a candidate gathering momentum to wrap up the nomination before the last region had voted. As such, the NASS plan does not guarantee every voter a meaningful voice in the primary, as a national primary does. And there is the possibility that the fortunate candidate whose region voted first would be the one getting a long head start on the rest of the field.

There is no mistaking that the rotating regional primary plan offers more dramatic change than natural evolution. While presently, many a state hold their presidential primary at a similar point of each election cycle, the NASS plan would tie states to their region like Ahab to Moby Dick, and force states to bounce around the spring calendar every four years.

Proponents of the plan, though, are hopeful that its sense of order and fairness will ultimately be convincing, and have not given up hope that it could be adopted by the parties in 2004 and implemented four years later. But by the summer of 2003, none of the plans—including that for rotating regional primaries—had gained much traction.

The "Delaware Plan:" The Choice of Republican Reformers

The national primary may be "the people's choice" and rotating regional primaries the choice of state election administrators, but the proposal that has come closest to winning acceptance in recent years is something called the "Delaware Plan."

It was the creation of the Delaware Republican Party, was recommended by a national GOP commission studying reform of the nominating process in the spring of 2000, and won approval from the Republican National Committee (RNC) that July. But shortly thereafter, the plan fell victim to convention politics in Philadelphia and was scuttled.

The Delaware Plan was a throwback to the back-loaded presidential primary calendar of a quarter century ago, when most of the primaries were held not in February and March, but May and June. The Delaware Plan called for states to be arranged in four groups according to population, with groups voting in inverse order of size at monthly intervals between March and June. The smallest states would vote first, the largest states last. With the large states holding nearly half the delegates, the reasoning went, there could be no rush to judgment since no candidate could realistically gain a majority of delegates until the final round of primaries was held in the spring.[7]

As a complement to the Delaware Plan, the GOP's advisory commission also recommended that the party eliminate winner-take-all in the awarding of delegates (which had existed for years in California, among other states) and require proportional representation, which would distribute delegates among all candidates receiving at least 15 percent of the primary or caucus vote. This change too, it was hoped, would help keep the nominating contest open into the last round of voting.

No special preference was extended to Iowa and New Hampshire under the Delaware Plan. In the plan's initial form, New Hampshire was just one of 12 states in the first group, which also included the District of Columbia, Puerto Rico and smaller territories such as American Samoa, Guam, and the Virgin Islands. Iowa was one of 13 states in the second group (see figure 6.2 and table 6.2).

Proponents of the Delaware Plan argued that the array of small states voting first would not only encourage more face to face campaigning by the candidates, but would level the playing field in the early going so that more candidates had a chance to compete. And by slowing down the resolution of the contest, they argued, more voters would have a meaningful voice. This plan would "make the presidential primary process more meaningful for more citizens," said RNC Chairman Jim Nicholson, than the "media-driven, front-loaded campaign process that disenfranchises so many states and so many voters."[8]

But the Delaware Plan had its critics as well, which attacked from different angles. Republican leaders in many of the larger states objected to being permanently relegated to the end of the primary calendar, where their role in the process would become problematic. Party "traditionalists' complained that the plan would shift power from the states to the national party. Democratic critics complained that the small states that would kick off the process were woefully lacking in racial diversity. Blacks and Hispanics combined to comprise only 10 percent of the population in the potpourri of small states and territories that would vote first, but totaled nearly 30 percent in the large states that would vote last.[9]

Other critics complained that the Delaware Plan would create a longer, more expensive campaign, as candidates would have to freneti-

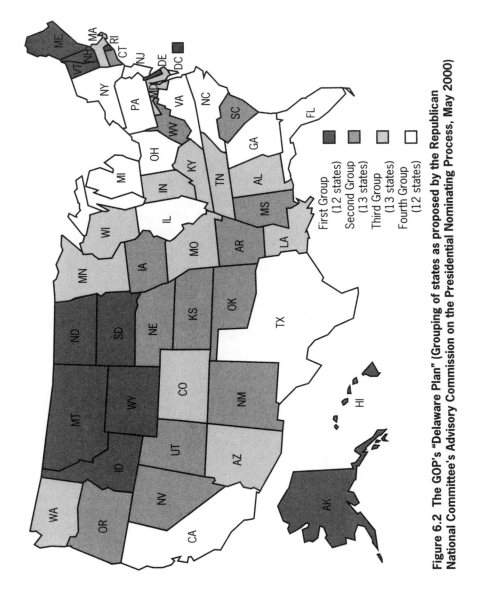

Figure 6.2 The GOP's "Delaware Plan" (Grouping of states as proposed by the Republican National Committee's Advisory Commission on the Presidential Nominating Process, May 2000)

Table 6.2.   The GOP's "Delaware Plan": And the Last Shall Be First

Republicans in 2000 strongly considered an overhaul of the presidential nominating process that would have arranged the states and territories into four groups according to population and have them vote at monthly intervals in inverse order—the smallest states first, the largest states last.

The Delaware Plan, as it was called, would have turned the current "front-loaded" primary calendar into a "back-loaded" one, so a candidate's ability to acquire a majority of delegates would have been slowed down considerably, enabling voters in the later primaries (it was hoped) to have a more meaningful voice in the nominating process.

The Delaware Plan ultimately was rejected by the 2000 GOP convention rules committee. But it had moved closer to realization than any other plan to reform the nominating process in recent years.

The chart below compares the number of Republican delegates that were actually selected by month from January to June 2000 with the number that would have been selected using the Delaware Plan. The plan initially called for states to vote from March to June, but was amended to move the calendar up a month so voting would take place from February to May. The amended version is reflected in this chart.

Percentage of Republican Delegates Selected by Month (2000)

Month	"Delaware Plan"	Actual
January	—	1%
February	12%	13%
March	17%	52%
April	23%	9%
May	47%	16%
June	—	8%

Source: Adapted from "Tentative 2000 Republican Presidential Primary/Caucus Dates" (RNC Counsel's Office, November 12, 1999); *New York Times*, May 3, 2000, A18.

cally hopscotch around the country to compete in the geographically far-flung groups of primaries.

With the prospect of a bitter fight on the floor of the Republican convention, the campaign of George W. Bush stepped in to kill the plan. Bush had been neutral on the issue, but with a vote on the proposal threatening to disrupt party harmony, Bush adviser Karl Rove was sent to tell key members of the convention rules committee that Bush wanted "no change" in the nominating process at that time. The Delaware Plan was subsequently scotched in the rules committee by a margin of 2-to-1.[10]

"I don't want the headlines to be about how we are going to elect a president in 2004," said Susan Weddington, a Texas GOP official. "I want them to be about electing this president." And with the defeat of the Delaware Plan, the Republican convention of 2000 was.[11]

145

NO CONSENSUS

The demise of the Delaware Plan illustrated the problem in making any dramatic change in the presidential nominating process. There are many players, many options, and consensus is difficult, if not impossible, to reach. And with changes in the past often producing unintended consequences, many politicians find it easiest to "just say no" to new calls for reform.

"Any proposal has problems," says New Hampshire Secretary of State Bill Gardner. And any proposal, even those with a modicum of support, must clear a variety of hurdles.[12]

Hurdles Galore

The Delaware Plan would have had to win approval from four different bodies within the Republican Party just to gain the GOP's stamp of approval. It cleared two of them—the rules committee of the RNC and the full committee itself—before crashing and burning on the eve of a broader review at the Philadelphia convention.

But even if the Delaware Plan had made it out of Philadelphia alive, its future was still uncertain. The next step would have been for the Republicans to reach agreement with the Democrats, so the two parties could present a united front to their state parties and the state legislatures.

That would have been difficult. Although both parties conducted separate reviews of the presidential nominating process at the beginning of the 2000 election cycle, and talked back and forth with each other in the process, they came to totally different conclusions about what to do. While the Republicans were willing to embrace dramatic reform, the Democrats opted for the status quo. Any plan for change is "fraught with potential problems far worse than the current system," the Democratic rules panel concluded.[13]

As such, the two parties reflected the conflicting attitudes that Americans have come to expect when reform of the nominating process is discussed. The "in" party, fresh off a presidential election victory or two, is much less interested in overhauling a process that has helped bring them victory. The "out" party, frustrated by defeat, is often more than willing to look at reform proposals.

Yet even if the Democrats and Republicans do ever end up on the same page, they are also separated by the matter of timing. Democrats revisit their party's nominating rules between elections. Republicans make decisions for the next four years at their national convention, so that any GOP-sanctioned change in the process for 2004 would have had to be approved by the Republican convention in 2000. Similarly, any change in the party's nominating process for 2008 would have to be approved by the 2004 GOP convention in New York.

Republicans did consider a party rules change in 2000 that would have given the RNC authority to draw up a new nominating process for 2004 between elections, ostensibly in league with the Democrats. But this proposal, like the Delaware Plan, was defeated by the convention rules committee. The only significant change that Republicans adopted for 2004 was the granting of automatic delegate seats to RNC members, creating for the first time a class of Republican "superdelegates."[14]

Congress could step in and impose a plan of its own on the parties. Legislators on Capitol Hill have already set the parameters for campaign finance in the nominating process, establishing the system of public financing coupled with spending and contribution limits. And plenty of proposals have been introduced in Congress over the years to reform the system of presidential primaries.

But it is not an area where many on Capitol Hill would like to go, nor would the parties like to see them do so. The courts over the years have underscored the right of the parties to fashion their own nominating processes. And many leading Democrats and Republicans believe the parties should continue to try to do just that. Says former RNC Chairman Rich Bond: "The parties should be strong enough to stand on their own."[15]

The Art of the Possible

In an effort to stem the front-loading of the primary calendar and increase voter participation, the parties will probably continue to experiment with ad hoc measures. But some of the most prominent of the recent past have enjoyed mixed success, at best.

There is the "window," the concept initiated by the Democrats in 1980 and since copied by the Republicans, which prohibits states from voting before a particular date. At first, the window opened the second Tuesday in March. In 2004, it will open the first Tuesday in February.

Then, there is the idea of bonus delegates for late-voting states, an experiment the Republicans adopted at their 1996 convention which found few takers among their state parties in 2000, and has since been rescinded.[16]

And the Democrats' requirement that all their publicly elected delegates be divided to reflect the primary or caucus vote did not keep the Democratic presidential contest alive in 2000 any longer than the Republican contest, where winner-take-all events are still allowed. The competitive stage of both contests ended the same day, March 9.

In terms of curbing front-loading and delaying the rush to judgment, all of these efforts have been futile—essentially about as effective as King Canute's command that the ocean tide recede.

Yet in terms of increasing voter participation, there may be room for creativity. Balloting by mail, the telephone, and by Internet have all been experimented with of late and could be used on a wider basis.

Oregon has conducted all its primary and general elections in recent years by mail. Voters literally have weeks to ponder their choices before returning their ballot. And though Oregon held its presidential primary in 2000 in May, long after the nominations had been decided, the primary turnout as a percentage of the presidential election turnout that fall was the seventh highest of any state in the country (46 percent). The ease of casting a ballot by mail had much to do with the respectable turnout. There were no lively gubernatorial or Senate primaries on the ballot to stir voter interest.[17]

North of the border, the leading opposition party, the Canadian Alliance, offered balloting by phone as an option to voting in person in their 2000 leadership selection primary. As noted in the last chapter, about half the party members who participated in the voting did so by phone.

In March 2000, Arizona Democrats experimented with Internet voting in their party-run presidential primary. Concerns were raised that the "digital divide" might work to the disadvantage of the state's large minority population of Hispanics, Indians and blacks. But several dozen Internet voting sites were established in communities with limited Internet access, as were some additional polling places.

Altogether, voters were given three options of voting in the primary—by paper ballot, by mail, or on the Internet. Ultimately, nearly half the 87,000 primary ballots were cast on the Internet, nearly 40 percent by mail, and the rest by traditional paper ballot at polling places.

Turnout for the Democratic presidential primary in Arizona was more than six times as high as 1996, when there was no Internet voting.[18]

A PARTING THOUGHT

Yet these are changes that tweak the nominating process around the edges. If the essence of a successful business is "location, location, location," the key to a wholesale increase in voter involvement in presidential primaries is "competition, competition, competition."

Election results in recent years have shown that if voters are given a meaningful choice, they will show up in goodly numbers. That is regularly the experience in New Hampshire, where the primary turnout approaches the size of a general election. Not every state can be a crossroads on the campaign trail as New Hampshire is. But a competitive choice could be offered voters in many, many more states than is currently the case.

Unfortunately, the goal of increased competition in the nominating process has run squarely into the parties' conflicting desire to end the primary contests as quickly and bloodlessly as possible. Of late, the latter desire has won out. Lengthy competition has given way to quick knockouts, denying millions of voters a meaningful voice.

There is a chance that another quick-ending nominating season in 2004 will bring the cry for reform to a critical mass, generating momentum behind one of the trio of plans, or maybe an entirely new one—that will overcome the current obstacles.

But don't bet on it. The smart money is not on any radical change, but a continuation of the gradually evolving system that is already in place—where the parties set the basic ground rules, the states have plenty of flexibility, and most of the voters have a role that is marginal at best.

Notes

CHAPTER 1: IS THERE A PLACE FOR US?

1. Data from Richard M. Scammon, Alice V. McGillivray, Rhodes Cook, *America Votes 24: A Handbook of Contemporary American Election Statistics* (Washington, D.C.: Congressional Quarterly Press, 2001), 42–45.

2. Rich Bond, interview with author, May 23, 2003.

CHAPTER 2: A PROCESS IN EVOLUTION: FROM THE FOUNDING FATHERS TO 1968

1. Roy F. Nichols, *The Invention of the American Political Parties* (New York: The Macmillan Company, 1967), 213.

2. *Presidential Elections 1789–1996* (Washington, D.C.: Congressional Quarterly Inc., 1997), 23. Since 1789, the Electoral College has been the formal mechanism for electing the president. Each state chooses electors equal to their total number of members in the House and the Senate. Even in the early years of the Republic, a few states allowed voters to pick the electors. In the rest, the state's legislature or executive branch selected them. Through the election of 1800, each elector had two votes. The candidate winning the highest number of votes from a majority of electors was elected president while the runner-up became vice president. However, the system nearly broke down in 1800, when both Thomas Jefferson and his running-mate, Aaron Burr, tied with 73 electoral votes. The election was thrown into the House of Representatives where Jefferson ultimately won a majority on the 36th ballot. After this episode, the 12th Amendment to the Constitution was passed, requiring the electors to vote separately for president and vice president.

3. Nichols, *American Political Parties*, 235.

151

4. Nichols, *American Political Parties*, 207, 226, 235.

5. Richard C. Bain and Judith H. Parris, *Convention Decisions and Voting Records* (Washington, D.C.: The Brookings Institution, 1973), 12.

6. Denis G. Sullivan, Jeffrey L. Pressman, and F. Christopher Arterton, *Explorations in Convention Decision Making* (San Francisco: W. H. Freeman and Company, 1976), 4.

7. *National Party Conventions 1831–2000* (Washington, D.C.: Congressional Quarterly Press, 2001), 20, 38.

8. *National Party Conventions*, 22, 24.

9. Nichols, *American Political Parties*, 354.

10. O. Key, Jr., *Politics, Parties & Pressure Groups* (New York: Thomas Y. Crowell Company, 1964), 372, 398. (5th Edition)

11. *National Party Conventions*, 39.

12. George H. Mayer, *The Republican Party 1854–1966* (New York: Oxford University Press, 1967), 67. (Second Edition)

13. Key, *Politics, Parties & Pressure Groups*, 398.

14. Carl Sandburg, *Abraham Lincoln: The Prairie Years* (New York: Dell Publishing Co., Inc., 1960), 288.

15. Paul W. Glad, *McKinley, Bryan and the People* (Philadelphia: J. B. Lippincott Company, 1964), 139.

16. Malcolm Moos, *The Republicans: A History of Their Party* (New York: Random House, 1956), 146.

17. Glad, *McKinley, Bryan*, 112.

18. Nichols, *American Political Parties*, 346.

19. Louise Overacker, *The Presidential Primary* (New York: The MacMillan Company, 1926), 13, 15–16.

20. James W. Davis, *Springboard to the White House: Presidential Primaries: How They are Fought and Won* (New York: Thomas Y. Crowell Company, 1967), 45–46.

21. John S. Jackson III, David H. Everson, Nancy L. Clayton, *The Making of a Primary: The Illinois Presidential Primary—1912–1992* (Springfield: Institute for Public Affairs, University of Illinois at Springfield, 1996), 11.

22. *New York Times*, April 11, 1912, 1.

23. Glad, *McKinley, Bryan*, 104.

24. Noel F. Busch, *TR* (New York: Reynal & Company, 1963), 267.

25. John L. Moore, Jon P. Preimesberger, David R. Tarr, eds., *Congressional Quarterly's Guide to U.S. Elections,* vol. I (Washington: Congressional Quarterly Press, 2001), 320–21. (4th Edition)

26. Mayer, *The Republican Party*, 328.

27. Bain and Parris, *Convention Decisions*, 181; *National Party Conventions*, 82.

28. Davis, *Springboard*, 201.

29. Overacker, *The Presidential Primary*, 251.

30. Donald Bruce Johnson and Kirk H. Porter (compilers), *National Party Platforms 1840–1972* (Urbana: University of Illinois Press, 1975), 170, 176. (5th Edition)

31. *National Party Conventions*, 22.

32. Overacker, *The Presidential Primary*, 13.

33. Davis, *Springboard*, 53–54.

34. Davis, *Springboard*, 207.

35. Robert K. Murray, *The 103rd Ballot: Democrats and the Disaster in Madison Square Garden* (New York: Harper & Row, 1976), 98.

36. Steve Neal, *Dark Horse: A Biography of Wendell Willkie* (Garden City, N.Y.: Doubleday & Company, Inc., 1984), 107–8; Bain and Parris, *Convention Decisions and Voting Records*, 252. The instant acceptance of public opinion polls was due in no small part to the massive failure of the huge straw vote conducted by the magazine, *Literary Digest*, in 1936. The millions of postal ballots counted by the *Digest* pointed to a victory for Republican nominee Alfred M. Landon, who ended up carrying only two states against FDR.

37. Neal, *Dark Horse*, 300.

38. Neal, *Dark Horse*, 303.

39. *Time*, April 17, 1944, 18–19.

40. *Time*, May 17, 1948, 24; *Newsweek*, May 31, 1948, 22.

41. *Newsweek*, March 31, 1952, 19.

42. Moos, *The Republicans*, 465–66.

43. Bain, *Convention Decisions*, 281–84.

44. *Newsweek*, March 24, 1952, 34.

45. *Time*, March 24, 1952, 20; Davis, *Springboard*, 115.

46. *Time*, April 18, 1960, 17.

47. Theodore H. White, *The Making of the President 1960* (New York: Atheneum, 1988), 107.

48. White, *Making of the President*, 112.

49. Davis, *Springboard*, 94.

50. Theodore H. White, *The Making of the President 1964* (New York: Atheneum, 1965), 128. Altogether, White wrote four books chronicling presidential campaigns from 1960 through 1972.

51. Davis, *Springboard*, 278–305; Rhodes Cook, *Race for the Presidency: Winning the 2000 Nomination* (Washington, D.C.: Congressional Quarterly Press, 2000), 50, 116, 120, 138.

52. Jules Witcover, *85 Days: The Last Campaign of Robert Kennedy* (New York: G. P. Putnam's Sons, 1969), 264; Lewis Chester, Godfrey Hodgson, Bruce Page, *An American Melodrama: The Presidential Campaign of 1968* (New York: Dell Publishing Co., Inc., 1969), 394.

CHAPTER 3: EVOLUTION SPEEDS UP:
THE MODERN ERA OF NOMINATING PRESIDENTS

1. Byron E. Shafer, *Quiet Revolution: The Struggle for the Democratic Party and the Shaping of Post-Reform Politics* (New York: Russell Sage Foundation, 1983), 35–36.

2. Shafer, *Quiet Revolution*, 73.

3. Shafer, *Quiet Revolution*, 112.

4. Austin Ranney, "Changing the Rules of the Presidential Nominating Game: Party Reform in America," *Parties and Elections*, 220.

5. Rhodes Cook, "National Conventions and Delegate Selection: An Overview," in *Parties and Elections in an Anti-Party Age: American Politics and the Crisis of Confidence*, ed. Jeff Fishel (Bloomington: Indiana University Press, 1978), 192, 196.

6. *Guide to the 1976 Democratic Convention* (Washington: Congressional Quarterly, 1976), 9. In 1976, the Democrats (but not the Republicans) abolished statewide winner-take-all primaries, such as the one that had existed for years in California. They installed a system of proportional representation, where delegates were distributed among candidates in a state or district (usually a congressional district) to reflect their share of the primary or caucus vote. This system is still used by the Democrats, though through 1984, several states were allowed to hold primaries with a direct vote for delegates, in which the winning candidate could end up taking all the delegates in a district. These contests were known as direct election, or "loophole," primaries. Democrats in a dozen states, including six of the 10 most populous, elected delegates in 1976 by this method.

7. Herbert E. Alexander, *Financing the 1976 Election* (Washington, D.C.: Congressional Quarterly Press, 1979), 13–14. Thomas B. Edsall, "Democrats Go to Bat With 2 Strikes," *Washington Post*, January 12, 2003, A4.

8. Cook, "National Conventions and Delegate Selection," 192.

9. Jonathan Moore and Janet Fraser, eds., *Campaign for President: The Managers Look at '76* (Cambridge, Mass.: Ballinger Publishing Company, 1977), 73.

10. Theodore H. White, *America in Search of Itself: The Making of the President 1956–1980* (New York: Harper & Row, 1982), 189.

11. Gerald R. Ford was chosen to be vice president by President Nixon in the fall of 1973 to replace Spiro T. Agnew, who resigned the post under an ethical cloud. As required by the 25th Amendment to the Constitution, Ford was confirmed as vice president by both chambers of Congress in separate votes taken before the end of 1973.

12. Moore and Fraser, *Campaign for President*, 69.

13. Lydia Saad, "When Presidential Frontrunners Emerge," *Public Perspective Magazine*, March/April 2000, 10.

14. Terry Michael, *The Democratic Party's Presidential Nominating Process: Fourth Edition * 2000 Convention* (Washington, D.C.: Washington Center for Politics & Journalism, 1999), 6–7.

15. Jack W. Germond and Jules Witcover, *Whose Broad Stripes and Bright Stars? The Trivial Pursuit of the Presidency 1988* (New York: Warner Books, 1989), 101.

16. William Schneider, "The November 4th Vote for President: What Did It Mean?" in Austin Ranney, ed., *The American Elections of 1980* (Washington, D.C.: American Enterprise Institute for Public Policy Research, 1981), 247.

17. White, *America in Search*, 303.

18. Paul R. Abramson, John H. Aldrich, and David W. Rohde, *Change and Continuity in the 1980 Elections* (Washington, D.C.: Congressional Quarterly Press, 1982), 20.

19. Jonathan Moore, ed., *The Campaign for President: 1980 In Retrospect* (Cambridge, Mass.: Ballinger Publishing Company, 1981), 49.

20. Jonathan Moore, ed., *Campaign for President: The Managers Look at '84* (Dover, Mass.: Auburn House Publishing Company, 1986), 88–89.

21. Adam Clymer, "The 1984 National Primary," *Public Opinion*, August/September 1984, 53.

22. Harold W. Stanley and Charles D. Hadley, "The Southern Presidential Primary: The Democratic Path to the Presidency?" (Rochester, N.Y.: Public Policy Analysis, University of Rochester, 1987), 5.

23. Earl Black and Merle Black, *The Vital South: How Presidents Are Elected* (Cambridge, Mass.: Harvard University Press, 1992), 285.

24. Black and Black, *Vital South*, 263. According to CBS/New York Times exit polls on March 8, 1988, the proportion of Democratic primary ballots cast by blacks in the five Southern states that Jesse Jackson carried ranged from 35 percent in Virginia to 45 percent in Alabama and Mississippi. In each contest, the percentage of blacks casting Democratic primary ballots was higher than the black share of the state population.

25. Charles T. Royer, ed., *Campaign for President: The Managers Look at '92* (Hollis, N.H.: Hollis Publishing Company), 57–58, 79.

26. Peter Goldman, Thomas M. DeFrank, Mark Miller, Andrew Murr, Tom Mathews, with Patrick Rogers and Melanie Cooper, *Quest for the Presidency 1992* (College Station: Texas A&M University, 1994), 340; Rhodes Cook, "Clinton, Brown Taste First Wins; Bush-Buchanan Duel Rolls On," *Congressional Quarterly Weekly Report*, March 7, 1992, 556.

27. That fall, Perot drew 19 percent of the popular vote—the most for any independent or third-party candidate since Theodore Roosevelt in 1912. Bush lost—the third president to be unseated in 16 years. Clinton won—but with only 43 percent of the popular vote, the fourth-lowest winning percentage for a victorious presidential candidate since the popular vote for president began being tallied in the early nineteenth century.

28. Larry J. Sabato, ed., *Toward the Millenium: The Elections of 1996* (Needham Heights, Mass.: Allyn & Bacon, 1997), 88, 236.

29. John L. Moore, Jon P. Preimesberger, and David R. Tarr, eds., *Congressional Quarterly's Guide to U.S. Elections*, Fourth Edition, Vol. 1 (Washington, D.C.: Congressional Quarterly Press, 2001), 22.

30. Moore, Preimesberger, and Tarr, eds., *Guide to U.S. Elections*, 420.

31. Larry J. Sabato, ed., *Overtime! The Election 2000 Thriller* (New York: Longman, 2002), 16.

32. Terry Michael, *Background and Explanation, Delegate Selection Rules, 2000 Democratic Convention* (Washington, D.C.: Washington Center for Politics & Journalism, 1999), 7.

33. David S. Broder, "GOP Scraps Plan to Alter Primary Schedule," *Washington Post*, July 29, 2000, A6.

34. David S. Broder, "Gephardt Criticizes 'Partisan' War Comments," *Washington Post*, January 20, 2002, A4.

CHAPTER 4: THE LAY OF THE LAND: 2004

1. Arthur T. Hadley, *The Invisible Primary* (Englewood Cliffs, N.J.: Prentice-Hall, Inc., 1976), 13.

2. Hadley, *Invisible Primary*, 14–20.

3. Jules Witcover, *Marathon: The Pursuit of the Presidency 1972–1976* (New York: The Viking Press, 1977), 127.

4. Theodore H. White, *America in Search of Itself: The Making of the President 1956–1980* (New York: Warner Books, 1982), 189; Witcover, *Marathon*, 199.

5. Rhodes Cook, "Carter Shows Surprising Strength in Iowa Poll," *Congressional Quarterly Weekly Report*, November 1, 1975, 2331.

6. George Bush with Victor Gold, *Looking Forward* (New York: Doubleday, 1987), 193–236; Emmett H. Buell, Jr., "The Invisible Primary," *In Pursuit of the White House: How We Choose Our Presidential Nominees*, William G. Mayer, ed. (Chatham, N.J.: Chatham House Publishers, Inc., 1996), 23.

7. "Behind the Straw Poll," *OnlineNewsHour*, August 13, 1999; Janine Yagielski, "They're off: Iowa straw poll sets GOP race in motion," *allpolitics.com*, August 15, 1999; "A behind-the-scenes look at the Iowa straw poll," *allpolitics.com*, August 15, 1999.

8. Essay by Emmett H. Buell Jr., "Presidential Primaries," *From the Founders to Front-Loading: Enduring Controversies in Presidential Nominating Politics*, Emmett H. Buell Jr. and William G. Mayer, eds. (forthcoming), chapter 15, 19–20.

9. "Delegate Selection Rules for the 2004 Democratic National Convention" (Washington, D.C.: Democratic National Committee, 2002), 12.

10. Susan Page, "Gore's back, and GOP is happier than Democrats," *USA Today*, November 19, 2002, 5A; "John Kerry Makes Two," editorial, *Washington Post*, December 3, 2002, A24.

11. Based on poll data provided the author by the Gallup Organization.

12. Buell, "The Invisible Primary," 13–15.

13. Thomas B. Edsall, "Democrats Go to Bat With 2 Strikes," *Washington Post*, January 12, 2003, A4.

14. "Financing the 1996 Presidential Campaign: Presidential Candidate Summary Report" on Federal Election Commission web site: www.fec.gov/pres96/presmstr.htm; "Receipts of 1999–2000 Presidential Campaigns Through July 31, 2000" on Federal Election Commission web site: www.fec.gov/finance/precm8.htm.

15. Don Van Natta Jr., "President Rewards 43 Members of Fund-Raising Club With Prominent Posts," *New York Times*, March 6, 2002, A18; Mike Allen, "Rangers Will Lead Bush's Fundraising Posse," *Washington Post*, May 24, 2003, A12.

16. Thomas B. Edsall, "Iowa Government Union Endorses Gore; UAW to Follow," *Washington Post*, June 26, 1999, A2.

17. David Yepsen, interview with author, January 27, 2003.

18. William G. Mayer, "The New Hampshire Primary: A Historical Overview," *Media and Momentum: The New Hampshire Primary and Nomination Politics,* Gary R. Orren and Nelson W. Polsby, eds. (Chatham, N.J.: Chatham House Publishers, Inc., 1987), 30; Rhodes Cook, *Race for the Presidency: Winning the 1988 Nomination* (Washington, D.C.: Congressional Quarterly Inc., 1987), 13; Rhodes Cook, "Steps to the Nomination," *Congressional Quarterly Weekly Report*, August 19, 1995, 2499.

19. Hugh Gregg, interview with author, January 14, 2003.

20. Mark Shields, interview with author, January 21, 2003.

21. Mark Shields, interview with author, January 21, 2003.

22. Glen Johnson, "Democrats look to test their mettle in Iowa caucuses," *Boston Globe*, October 6, 2002, A6.

23. Mark Shields, "Most influential primary," Creators Syndicate, posted January 13, 2003.

24. "Back Into the Mosh Pit," analysis of Republican primary voting through February 22, 2000 at www.rhodescook.com/analysis.html. Based on author's findings through extrapolation of primary vote using exit poll data.

25. "Delegate Selection Rules for the 2004 Democratic National Convention" (Washington, D.C.: Democratic National Committee, 2002), 3. Phil McNamara, interview with author, January 13, 2003.

26. Gregory L. Giroux, "Mark Your Calendar for the 2004 Race," *Congressional Quarterly Weekly*, December 14, 2002, 3230; Dan Balz, "Mich. Cau-

cuses May Rival Early Races in Iowa, N.H.," *Washington Post,* March 2, 2003, A4; Craig Timberg, "D.C. Sets Presidential Primary Ahead of States'," *Washington Post*, March 5, 2003, B4.

27. Rhodes Cook, *Race for the Presidency: Winning the 2000 Nomination* (Washington, D.C.: CQ Press, 2000), viii.

28. Mark Shields, interview with author, January 21, 2003.

29. Exit poll data for the November 2000 presidential election is from *The New York Times*, November 12, 2000, IV, 4. Exit poll data from the early 2000 presidential primaries and caucuses: Iowa: cnn.com/ELECTION/2000/primaries/IA/poll.html; New Hampshire: www.msnbc.com/m/d2k/nh_p_d.asp; www.msnbc.com/m/d2k/nh_p_r.asp; South Carolina: cnn.com/ELECTION/2000/primaries/SC/poll.rep.html; Michigan: cnn.com/ELECTION/2000/primaries/MI/results.rep.html.

30. Adam Clymer, "The 1984 National Primary," *Public Opinion*, August/September 1984, 52–53; "A Recap of the Primaries: How the Democrats Voted," *New York Times*, June 13, 1988, B7; "Recap of the Primaries: How Democrats in 29 States Voted," *New York Times*, July 12, 1992, 18.

31. Austin Ranney, interview with author, January 27, 2003.

32. Exit poll data for the November 2000 presidential election is from *The New York Times*, November 12, 2000, IV, 4. Exit poll data from the early 2000 presidential primaries and caucuses: Iowa: cnn.com/ELECTION/2000/primaries/IA/poll.html; New Hampshire: www.msnbc.com/m/d2k/nh_p_d.asp; www.msnbc.com/m/d2k/nh_p_r.asp; South Carolina: cnn.com/ELECTION/2000/primaries/SC/poll.rep.html; Michigan: cnn.com/ELECTION/2000/primaries/MI/results.rep.html.

33. Adam Clymer, "The 1984 National Primary," *Public Opinion*, August/September 1984, 52–3; "A Recap of the Primaries: How the Democrats Voted," *New York Times*, June 13, 1988, B7; "Recap of the Primaries: How Democrats in 29 States Voted," *New York Times*, July 12, 1992, 18.

34. From appearance on CNBC's "Tim Russert Show," February 15, 2003.

35. David Yepsen, interview with author, January 27, 2003.

36. Martin Plissner, *The Control Room: How Television Calls the Shots in Presidential Elections* (New York: The Free Press, 1999), 46.

37. Missouri has voted for the victorious presidential candidate in every election since 1904 with one exception—1956—when it went for Democrat Adlai Stevenson over Republican incumbent Dwight Eisenhower.

CHAPTER 5: LOOKING TO THE WORLD: HOW OTHER COUNTRIES SELECT THEIR LEADERS

1. James W. Davis, *Leadership Selection in Six Western Democracies* (Westport, Conn.: Greenwood Press, 1998), 9–11.

2. Davis, *Leadership Selection*, 6, 179.

3. Dean McSweeney, *Changing the Rules Changed the Game, Selecting Conservative Leaders in Party Politics* (London: Sage Publications, 1999).

4. "Stirring up the party faithful," *The Economist*, October 11, 1997, 67–68; Davis, *Leadership Selection*, 78.

5. Keith Alderman and Neil Carter, "The Labour Party Leadership and Deputy Leadership Elections of 1994," *Parliamentary Affairs*, Vol. 48 (July 1995), 445.

6. Alderman and Carter, "The Labour Party Leadership and Deputy Leadership Elections of 1994," 443.

7. Alderman and Carter, "The Labour Party Leadership and Deputy Leadership Elections of 1994," 449, 452.

8. Alderman and Carter, "The Labour Party Leadership and Deputy Leadership Elections of 1994," 449, 452; Davis, *Leadership Selection*, 97.

9. George F. Will, "Tories at the Continental Divide," *Washington Post*, September 6, 2001, A23.

10. Keith Alderman and Neil Carter, "The Conservative Party Leadership Election of 2001," *Parliamentary Affairs*, Vol. 55 (July 2002), 580–81.

11. Nicholas Watt, "It's war as Major takes on Thatcher over leadership," *The Guardian*, August 22, 2001, from web site: politics.guardian.co.uk/conservatives/story/0,9061,540590.00.html; Warren Hoge, "British Conservatives Choose 'Euroskeptic' Leader; Facing Fractious Party, *New York Times*, September 14, 2001, B1.

12. Warren Hoge, "An Uncommonly Spirited Campaign Roils British Tories," *New York Times*, July 28, 2001, A3; Alderman and Carter, "The Conservative Party Leadership Election of 2001," 581, 583.

13. Suzanne Daley, "In Underwhelming Turnout, French Voters Cut Presidential Term," *New York Times*, September 25, 2000, A3.

14. Davis, *Leadership Selection*, 134.

15. John Tagliabue, "France's First-Round Presidential Ballot Takes Shape," *New York Times*, April 3, 2002, A3.

16. David Buchan, "French Socialists seek a gallant loser," *Financial Times*, February 3, 1995, 2.

17. Davis, *Leadership Selection*, 149.

18. Keith B. Richburg, "Unhappy Voters Turn to Chirac," *Washington Post*, May 4, 2002, A18.

19. Richburg, "Unhappy Voters Turn to Chirac," A18.

20. Jim Hoagland, "Le Pen: An Electoral Mess . . . ," *Washington Post*, April 23, 2002, A19; "Chirac's coalition heads for control of parliament," *USA Today*, June 10, 2002, 7A.

21. E.J. Dionne, ". . . A Colossal Bungle," *Washington Post*, April 23, 2002, A17.

22. Davis, *Leadership Selection*, 181–82. The last two German chancellors, Gerhard Schroeder and Helmut Kohl, were previously minister-presidents of German states: Kohl of Rhineland-Palatinate, Schroeder of Lower Saxony. Two of the first chancellors were former mayors, Konrad Adenauer of Cologne and Willy Brandt of West Berlin.

23. Davis, *Leadership Selection*, 186.

24. *Facts on File*, March 5, 1998, 135–36.

25. Peter Finn, "Bavarian Is Chosen To Oppose Schroeder," *Washington Post*, January 12, 2002, A16.

26. Neal E. Boudette, "Schroder Is Narrowly Re-Elected," *Wall Street Journal*, September 23, 2002, A3.

27. Davis, *Leadership Selection*, 43.

28. Davis, *Leadership Selection*, 49.

29. Davis, *Leadership Selection*, 47.

30. Davis, *Leadership Selection*, 60–61.

31. John H. Fund, "Northern Exposure: Canada's Politics Open Up," *Wall Street Journal*, June 16, 2000, A15; James Brooke, "Conservatives In Canada Select Leader of New Party," *New York Times*, June 26, 2000, A6; James Brooke, "After Election Risk, Premier of Canada Reaps Big Rewards," *New York Times*, November 29, 2000, A6.

32. Terry Horkoff, executive director of the Canadian Alliance Party, interview with author, May 15, 2003.

33. Davis, *Leadership Selection*, 65; Tom Cohen, "Chretien Sets His Departure For 2004," *Washington Post*, August 22, 2002, A10.

34. Joel Baglole, "Canada's Chretien Faces a Leadership Challenge From Within," *Wall Street Journal*, August 6, 2002, A18.

35. Sam Dillon, "Zedillo Suggests U.S.-Style System to Pick Nominees," *New York Times*, March 5, 1999, A1.

36. George Grayson, *A Guide to the November 7, 1999, PRI Presidential Primary, including data on the PRI Primary in Mexico City*, Western Hemisphere Election Study Series Volume XVII, Study 4, CSIS (Center for Strategic and International Studies), October 1999, 3.

37. *Facts on File*, November 18, 1999, 843.

38. Julia Preston, "With Vote, Mexican Right Gives a Hand To Candidate," *New York Times*, September 13, 1999, A3.

39. *Associated Press*, November 28, 2002.

40. Joel Greenberg, "Netanyahu Vows to Oust Arafat If Elected," *New York Times,* November 13, 2002, A6.

41. James Bennett, "As Israel Faces Violence Abroad, Likud Chooses Sharon," *New York Times*, November 30, 2002, A11.

42. Molly Moore and John Ward Anderson, "Six Slain at Israeli Polling Station," *Washington Post*, November 29, 2002, A1, A47.

43. *Agence France Press*, November 17, 20, 2002.

44. Lee Hockstader, "Vote Dispute Divides Israel's Labor Party," *Washington Post*, September 6, 2001, A20.

45. Clyde Haberman, "Israeli Party Is Bickering After Near-Tie In Its Primary," *New York Times*, September 6, 2001, A9; James Bennet, "Vote in Israel In Labor Party Seems to Keep Coalition Safe," *New York Times*, December 27, 2001, A7.

CHAPTER 6: CAN WE DO BETTER THAN THIS?

1. "A Review of the Republican Process: Nominating Future Presidents" (Advisory Commission on the Presidential Nominating Process; A Report Commissioned by the Republican National Committee, 2000), 44–48.

2. "2004 Presidential Primary Calendar" (as of May 5, 2003) on National Association of Secretaries of State (NASS) web site: www.nass.org/Issues/04primaries.html

3. Based on poll data provided the author by the Gallup Organization.

4. Michael Nelson, "Two Cheers for the National Primary," in Emmett H. Buell, Jr. and William G. Mayer, coeditors, *From the Founders to Front-Loading: Enduring Controversies in Presidential Nominating Politics* (unpublished), 8–9.

5. Based on poll data provided by the Gallup Organization. The Gallup Poll of "Opinion Leaders" was taken in August 1982, and showed 47 percent in favor of a nationwide primary election and 42 percent opposed. According to the Gallup Organization, the sample of 1,346 "Opinion Leaders" included the "nation's most prominent citizens, including university presidents, scientists, statesmen, clergy, business and labor leaders, and prominent persons in many other fields."

6. "NASS Presidential Primary Plan," as found on the web site of the National Association of Secretaries of State (NASS): www.nass.org/issue.html

7. *Associated Press*, "Overhaul of GOP Primaries Backed," *Washington Post*, May 13, 2000, A10. At a meeting in May 2000, the rules committee of the Republican National Committee changed the time frame of the "Delaware Plan" from February to May, moving the entire schedule up one month.

8. Adam Clymer, "G.O.P. Panel Sets Vote on Revising Primaries," *New York Times*, May 13, 2000, A24.

9. "RNC Primary Commission Recommends Changes to Enhance Voter Participation in Presidential Nominating System," *RNC News* press release, May 2, 2000.

10. David S. Broder, "GOP Scraps Plan to Alter Primary Schedule," *Washington Post*, July 29, 2000, A6.

11. *Associated Press*, "Overhaul of GOP Primaries Backed," *Washington Post*, May 13, 2000, A10.

12. Bill Gardner, interview with author, May 23, 2003.

13. *Election Administration Reports* (Vol. 30, No.10), May 15, 2000, 6. The Democratic review of the presidential nominating process was undertaken by the Democratic National Committee's Rules and Bylaws Committee. Their conclusions were included in a report issued in April 2000 titled "Beyond 2000: The Scheduling of Future Democratic Primaries and Caucuses."

14. "The Rules of the Republican Party As Adopted by the 2000 Republican National Convention July 31, 2000," on Republican National Committee web site: www.rnc.org/2000/goprules; David S. Broder, "GOP Scraps Plan to Alter Primary Schedule," *Washington Post*, July 29, 2000, A6.

15. Rich Bond, interview with author, May 23, 2003.

16. "The Rules of the Republican Party As Adopted by the 2000 Republican National Convention July 31, 2000," on Republican National Committee web site: www.rnc.org/2000/goprules.

17. Rhodes Cook, *Race for the Presidency: Winning the 2000 Nomination* (Washington, D.C.: CQ Press, 2000), 124.

18. Robert S. Done, "Internet Voting: Bringing Elections to the Desktop," *E-Government Series* (The PricewaterhouseCoopers Endowment for The Business of Government), February 2002, 6–8. In Arizona's 2000 Democratic presidential balloting, off-site Internet voting was allowed over a four-day span from March 7 through 10. Polling places, where paper and Internet ballots could be cast, were open on March 11. Bill Bradley was a candidate during the opening days of the Arizona voting. He withdrew from the Democratic presidential race on March 9, leaving Al Gore unopposed after that. Bill Clinton ran without opposition in Arizona's 1996 Democratic presidential primary.

Index

About the Author

Rhodes Cook has covered presidential and congressional elections for more than a quarter century—as a political writer for *Congressional Quarterly* from 1975 through 1997; since then as author of "The Rhodes Cook Letter," the host of a political website, and as a contributing editor for *Public Perspective*. Since 1996, he has been the author of *America Votes* (a biennial compilation of nationwide election data) and has written several books on the presidential nominating process, most recently *United States Presidential Primary Elections 1968–1996: A Handbook of Election Statistics* and *Race for the Presidency: Winning the 2000 Nomination*. He lives in Annandale, Virginia, with his wife, Memrie.